Get Ready!

FOR STANDARDIZED TESTS

Other Books in the *Get Ready!* Series:

Get Ready! for Standardized Tests: Grade 2 by Joseph Harris, Ph.D.

Get Ready! for Standardized Tests: Grade 3 by Karen Mersky, Ph.D.

Get Ready! for Standardized Tests: Grade 4 by Joseph Harris, Ph.D.

Get Ready! for Standardized Tests: Grade 5 by Leslie E. Talbott, Ph.D.

Get Ready! for Standardized Tests: Grade 6 by Shirley Vickery, Ph.D.

TEST PREPARATION SERIES

Get Ready!

FOR STANDARDIZED TESTS

GRADE ONE

Joseph Harris, Ph.D.

Carol Turkington
Series Editor

McGraw-Hill

New York   San Francisco Washington, D.C. Auckland Bogotá
Caracas Lisbon London Madrid Mexico City Milan
Montreal New Delhi San Juan Singapore
Sydney Tokyo Toronto

Library of Congress Cataloging-in-Publication Data

Get ready! for standardized tests / c Carol Turkington, series editor.
    p. cm.
    Includes bibliographical references.
    Contents: [1] Grade 1 / Joseph Harris — [2] Grade 2 / Joseph Harris — [3] Grade 3 /
Karen Mersky — [4] Grade 4 / Joseph Harris — [5] Grade 5 / Leslie E. Talbott — [6]
Grade 6 / Shirley Vickery.
    ISBN 0-07-136010-7 (v. 1) — ISBN 0-07-136011-5 (v. 2) — ISBN 0-07-136012-3 (v. 3)
— ISBN 0-07-136013-1 (v. 4) — ISBN 0-07-136014-X (v. 5) — ISBN 0-07-136015-8 (v. 6)
    1. Achievement tests—United States—Study guides.   2. Education, Elementary—United
States—Evaluation.   3. Education, Elementary—Parent participation—United States.   I.
Turkington, Carol.   II. Harris, Joseph.

LB3060.22 .G48   2000
372.126—dc21   00-056083

McGraw-Hill

A Division of The McGraw·Hill Companies

1 2 3 4 5 6 7 8 9 0 PBT/PBT 0 9 8 7 6 5 4 3 2 1 0

ISBN 0-07-136010-7

This book was set in New Century Schoolbook by Inkwell Publishing Services.

Printed and bound by Phoenix Book Technology.

McGraw-Hill books are available at special quantity discounts to use as premiums and sales pro-
motions, or for use in corporate training programs. For more information, please write to the
Director of Special Sales, McGraw-Hill, Professional Publishing, Two Penn Plaza, New York,
NY 10121-2298. Or contact your local bookstore.

To my son, Ross Adam Harris

Contents

CONTENTS

SKILLS CHECKLIST

MY CHILD ...	HAS LEARNED	IS WORKING ON
WORD ANALYSIS		
Letter recognition		
Beginning sounds		
Ending sounds		
Rhyming sounds		
Word recognition		
Sight words		
Vowel sounds		
Word study		
VOCABULARY		
Picture vocabulary		
Sight vocabulary		
Receptive vocabulary		
Expressive vocabulary		
Word meaning		
Synonyms		
Antonyms		
Words in context		
READING COMPREHENSION		
Listening comprehension		
Picture comprehension		
Sentence comprehension		
Story comprehension		
LISTENING		
Sustained listening		
Active listening		
Language skills		
LANGUAGE MECHANICS		
Capitalization		
Punctuation		
Usage		
Pronouns		
Sentences		
Paragraphs		
SPELLING		
Vowels		
Consonants		
Spelling		
MATH CONCEPTS		
Numeration		
Sequencing		
Number concepts		
Patterns		
Place value		
MATH COMPUTATION		
Addition		
Subtraction		
MATH APPLICATIONS		
Shapes		
Geometry		
Measurement		
Word problems		

Introduction

Almost all of us have taken standardized tests in school. We spent several days bubbling-in answers, shifting in our seats. No one ever told us why we took the tests or what they would do with the results. We just took them and never heard about them again.

Today many parents aren't aware they are entitled to see their children's permanent records and, at a reasonable cost, to obtain copies of any information not protected by copyright, including testing scores. Late in the school year, most parents receive standardized test results with confusing bar charts and detailed explanations of scores that few people seem to understand.

In response to a series of negative reports on the state of education in this country, Americans have begun to demand that something be done to improve our schools. We have come to expect higher levels of accountability as schools face the competing pressures of rising educational expectations and declining school budgets. High-stakes standardized tests are rapidly becoming the main tool of accountability for students, teachers, and school administrators. If students' test scores don't continually rise, teachers and principals face the potential loss of school funding and, ultimately, their jobs. Summer school and private after-school tutorial program enrollments are swelling with students who have not met score standards or who, everyone agrees, could score higher.

While there is a great deal of controversy about whether it is appropriate for schools to use standardized tests to make major decisions about individual students, it appears likely that standardized tests are here to stay. They will be used to evaluate students, teachers, and the schools; schools are sure to continue to use students' test scores to demonstrate their accountability to the community.

The purposes of this guide are to acquaint you with the types of standardized tests your children may take; to help you understand the test results; and to help you work with your children in skill areas that are measured by standardized tests so they can perform as well as possible.

Types of Standardized Tests

The two major types of group standardized tests are *criterion-referenced tests* and *norm-referenced tests*. Think back to when you learned to tie your shoes. First Mom or Dad showed you how to loosen the laces on your shoe so that you could insert your foot; then they showed you how to tighten the laces—but not too tight. They showed you how to make bows and how to tie a knot. All the steps we just described constitute what is called a *skills hierarchy:* a list of skills from easiest to most difficult that are related to some goal, such as tying a shoelace.

Criterion-referenced tests are designed to determine at what level students are performing on various skills hierarchies. These tests assume that development of skills follows a sequence of steps. For example, if you were teaching shoelace tying, the skills hierarchy might appear this way:

1. Loosen laces.
2. Insert foot.
3. Tighten laces.
4. Make loops with both lace ends.
5. Tie a square knot.

Criterion-referenced tests try to identify how far along the skills hierarchy the student has progressed. There is no comparison against anyone else's score, only against an expected skill level. The main question criterion-referenced tests ask is: "Where is this child in the development of this group of skills?"

Norm-referenced tests, in contrast, are typically constructed to compare children in their abilities as to different skills areas. Although the experts who design test items may be aware of skills hierarchies, they are more concerned with how much of some skill the child has mastered, rather than at what level on the skills hierarchy the child is.

Ideally, the questions on these tests range from very easy items to those that are impossibly difficult. The essential feature of norm-referenced tests is that scores on these measures can be compared to scores of children in similar groups. They answer this question: "How does the child compare with other children of the same age or grade placement in the development of this skill?"

This book provides strategies for increasing your child's scores on both standardized norm-referenced and criterion-referenced tests.

The Major Standardized Tests

Many criterion-referenced tests currently in use are created locally or (at best) on a state level,

and there are far too many of them to go into detail here about specific tests. However, children prepare for them in basically the same way they do for norm-referenced tests.

A very small pool of norm-referenced tests is used throughout the country, consisting primarily of the Big Five:

- California Achievement Tests (CTB/McGraw-Hill)
- Iowa Tests of Basic Skills (Riverside)
- Metropolitan Achievement Test (Harcourt-Brace & Company)
- Stanford Achievement Test (Psychological Corporation)
- TerraNova [formerly Comprehensive Test of Basic Skills] (McGraw-Hill)

These tests use various terms for the academic skills areas they assess, but they generally test several types of reading, language, and mathematics skills, along with social studies and science. They may include additional assessments, such as of study and reference skills.

How States Use Standardized Tests

Despite widespread belief and practice to the contrary, group standardized tests are designed to assess and compare the achievement of groups. They are *not* designed to provide detailed diagnostic assessments of individual students. (For detailed individual assessments, children should be given individual diagnostic tests by properly qualified professionals, including trained guidance counselors, speech and language therapists, and school psychologists.) Here are examples of the types of questions group standardized tests are designed to answer:

- How did the reading achievement of students at Valley Elementary School this year compare with their reading achievement last year?

- How did math scores at Wonderland Middle School compare with those of students at Parkside Middle School this year?

- As a group, how did Hilltop High School students compare with the national averages in the achievement areas tested?

- How did the district's first graders' math scores compare with the district's fifth graders' math scores?

The fact that these tests are designed primarily to test and compare groups doesn't mean that test data on individual students isn't useful. It does mean that when we use these tests to diagnose individual students, we are using them for a purpose for which they were not designed.

Think of group standardized tests as being similar to health fairs at the local mall. Rather than check into your local hospital and spend thousands of dollars on full, individual tests for a wide range of conditions, you can go from station to station and take part in different health screenings. Of course, one would never diagnose heart disease or cancer on the basis of the screening done at the mall. At most, suspicious results on the screening would suggest that you need to visit a doctor for a more complete examination.

In the same way, group standardized tests provide a way of screening the achievement of many students quickly. Although you shouldn't diagnose learning problems solely based on the results of these tests, the results can tell you that you should think about referring a child for a more definitive, individual assessment.

An individual student's group test data should be considered only a point of information. Teachers and school administrators may use standardized test results to support or question hypotheses they have made about students; but these scores must be used alongside other information, such as teacher comments, daily work, homework, class test grades, parent observations, medical needs, and social history.

Valid Uses of Standardized Test Scores

Here are examples of appropriate uses of test scores for individual students:

- Mr. Cone thinks that Samantha, a third grader, is struggling in math. He reviews her file and finds that her first- and second-grade standardized test math scores were very low. Her first- and second-grade teachers recall episodes in which Samantha cried because she couldn't understand certain math concepts, and mention that she was teased by other children, who called her "Dummy." Mr. Cone decides to refer Samantha to the school assistance team to determine whether she should be referred for individual testing for a learning disability related to math.

- The local college wants to set up a tutoring program for elementary school children who are struggling academically. In deciding which youngsters to nominate for the program, the teachers consider the students' averages in different subjects, the degree to which students seem to be struggling, parents' reports, and standardized test scores.

- For the second year in a row, Gene has performed poorly on the latest round of standardized tests. His teachers all agree that Gene seems to have some serious learning problems. They had hoped that Gene was immature for his class and that he would do better this year; but his dismal grades continue. Gene is referred to the school assistance team to determine whether he should be sent to the school psychologist for assessment of a possible learning handicap.

Inappropriate Use of Standardized Test Scores

Here are examples of how schools have sometimes used standardized test results inappropriately:

- Mr. Johnson groups his students into reading groups solely on the basis of their standardized test scores.

- Ms. Henry recommends that Susie be held back a year because she performed poorly on the standardized tests, despite strong grades on daily assignments, homework, and class tests.

- Gerald's teacher refers him for consideration in the district's gifted program, which accepts students using a combination of intelligence test scores, achievement test scores, and teacher recommendations. Gerald's intelligence test scores were very high. Unfortunately, he had a bad cold during the week of the standardized group achievement tests and was taking powerful antihistamines, which made him feel sleepy. As a result, he scored too low on the achievement tests to qualify.

The public has come to demand increasingly high levels of accountability for public schools. We demand that schools test so that we have hard data with which to hold the schools accountable. But too often, politicians and the public place more faith in the test results than is justified. Regardless of whether it's appropriate to do so and regardless of the reasons schools use standardized test results as they do, many schools base crucial programming and eligibility decisions on scores from group standardized tests. It's to your child's advantage, then, to perform as well as possible on these tests.

Two Basic Assumptions

The strategies we present in this book come from two basic assumptions:

1. Most students can raise their standardized test scores.

2. Parents can help their children become stronger in the skills the tests assess.

This book provides the information you need to learn what skill areas the tests measure, what general skills your child is being taught in a particular grade, how to prepare your child to take the tests, and what to do with the results. In the appendices you will find information to help you decipher test interpretations; a listing of which states currently require what tests; and additional resources to help you help your child to do better in school and to prepare for the tests.

A Word about Coaching

This guide is *not* about coaching your child. When we use the term *coaching* in referring to standardized testing, we mean trying to give someone an unfair advantage, either by revealing beforehand what exact items will be on the test or by teaching "tricks" that will supposedly allow a student to take advantage of some detail in how the tests are constructed.

Some people try to coach students in shrewd test-taking strategies that take advantage of how the tests are supposedly constructed rather than strengthening the students' skills in the areas tested. Over the years, for example, many rumors have been floated about "secret formulas" that test companies use.

This type of coaching emphasizes ways to help students obtain scores they didn't earn—to get something for nothing. Stories have appeared in the press about teachers who have coached their students on specific questions, parents who have tried to obtain advance copies of tests, and students who have written down test questions after taking standardized tests and sold them to others. Because of the importance of test security, test companies and states aggressively prosecute those who attempt to violate test security—and they should do so.

How to Raise Test Scores

Factors that are unrelated to how strong students are but that might artificially lower test scores include anything that prevents students from making scores that accurately describe their actual abilities. Some of those factors are:

- giving the tests in uncomfortably cold or hot rooms;

- allowing outside noises to interfere with test taking; and

- reproducing test booklets in such small print or with such faint ink that students can't read the questions.

Such problems require administrative attention from both the test publishers, who must make sure that they obtain their norms for the tests under the same conditions students face when they take the tests; and school administrators, who must ensure that conditions under which their students take the tests are as close as possible to those specified by the test publishers.

Individual students also face problems that can artificially lower their test scores, and parents can do something about many of these problems. Stomach aches, headaches, sleep deprivation, colds and flu, and emotional upsets due to a recent tragedy are problems that might call for the student to take the tests during make-up sessions. Some students have physical conditions such as muscle-control problems, palsies, or difficulty paying attention that require work over many months or even years before students can obtain accurate test scores on standardized tests. And, of course, some students just don't take the testing seriously or may even intentionally perform poorly. Parents can help their children overcome many of these obstacles to obtaining accurate scores.

Finally, with this book parents are able to help their children raise their scores by:

- increasing their familiarity (and their comfort level) with the types of questions on standardized tests;

- drills and practice exercises to increase their skill in handling the kinds of questions they will meet; and

- providing lots of fun ways for parents to help their children work on the skill areas that will be tested.

Test Questions

The favorite type of question for standardized tests is the multiple-choice question. For example:

1. The first President of the United States was:

   A Abraham Lincoln

   B Martin Luther King, Jr.

   C George Washington

   D Thomas Jefferson

The main advantage of multiple-choice questions is that it is easy to score them quickly and accurately. They lend themselves to optical scanning test forms, on which students fill in bubbles or squares and the forms are scored by machine. Increasingly, companies are moving from paper-based testing to computer-based testing, using multiple-choice questions.

The main disadvantage of multiple-choice questions is that they restrict test items to those that can be put in that form. Many educators and civil rights advocates have noted that the multiple-choice format only reveals a superficial understanding of the subject. It's not possible with multiple-choice questions to test a student's ability to construct a detailed, logical argument on some issue or to explain a detailed process. Although some of the major tests are beginning to incorporate more subjectively scored items, such as short answer or essay questions, the vast majority of test items continue to be in multiple-choice format.

In the past, some people believed there were special formulas or tricks to help test-takers determine which multiple-choice answer was the correct one. There may have been some truth to *some* claims for past tests. Computer analyses of some past tests revealed certain biases in how tests were constructed. For example, the old advice to pick *D* when in doubt appears to have been valid for some past tests. However, test publishers have become so sophisticated in their ability to detect patterns of bias in the formulation of test questions and answers that they now guard against it aggressively.

In Chapter 1, we provide information about general test-taking considerations, with advice on how parents can help students overcome testing obstacles. The rest of the book provides information to help parents help their children strengthen skills in the tested areas.

Joseph Harris, Ph.D.

Test-Taking Basics

Before we turn to specific strategies for taking tests, we need to understand the nature of a first-grade child. It's no accident that most cultures begin a child's formal academic studies by about age 6. Although most North American children have already had at least one year of kindergarten by age 6, first grade is when the emphasis on academics usually begins.

A First Grader's Development

By the end of first grade, a child's brain is about 90 percent of its adult weight; the areas of the brain that govern reading, language, and mathematics have grown to the point that children can begin direct instruction in academic skills such as reading, writing, and math. As the 6-year-old's brain continues to mature, parents who were frustrated because they wondered if little Johnny would ever learn the alphabet or little Janey would ever learn left from right begin to see their children abruptly develop those skills.

One of the most serious though well-intentioned mistakes parents of first graders make is to struggle to get their children to master skills for which they aren't neurologically ready. For example, although most children at this age are ready to learn to read, some just aren't. No amount of pressure will make them ready to read.

It's fine to help your child develop academic skills, but if you find you're trying to teach the same skills over and over and your child just isn't getting it, perhaps you are trying to teach a skill for which your child isn't yet ready.

Moving the Body

Almost all children have decided whether they are left- or right-handed by this age, although some may still switch from one to the other, such as writing with one hand but drawing with the other. Compared with older children, many 6-year-olds seem to be somewhat clumsy. They may have some problems staying within lines when coloring, and they may have problems keeping their eyes on the same line when reading. But they are growing steadily stronger and better coordinated and are developing a much stronger awareness of their body positions and movement.

How They Think

The late Swiss developmental psychologist Jean Piaget spent decades observing children at different ages and noting changes in their learning abilities. His theories about how children learn have had a major influence on Western education. According to Piaget, the child entering first grade tends to be very intuitive; that is, he tends to be influenced more by what he feels than by what logic tells him. Jamie may argue with his last breath that all snakes are poisonous, and no amount of logic may convince him otherwise. When his father asks how he knows this, he responds, "I just do." Children at this age have acquired many skills, but they can't describe how they acquired them. They "just know."

Symbolic reasoning also begins to emerge at this age, as children begin to recognize the squiggly lines on the page that stand for *apple* and others that stand for the number *four*. The development of the ability to think in terms of symbols is what allows most children to begin to learn to read at about age 6.

First graders also begin to develop much more flexible classification skills: When presented with pictures of a boat, an automobile, and a bicycle and asked to tell how these things are alike, many younger children will state with conviction that they are alike because they are all green or that they are all good. The concept that they are similar (they are modes of transportation) may not occur to them until about first grade. You will notice your 6-year-old becoming more able to recognize abstract qualities and to consider more than one characteristic at a time.

Emotions and Behavior

Many first graders are simply not prepared to sit still and concentrate for an entire school day. They would prefer to be running through leaves and playing with the dog instead of sitting at their desks. Even children who don't have attention deficit disorders may find paying attention to be a very difficult thing. Children at this age also view "I don't want to" as a legitimate reason for not doing things that they find boring or unpleasant. They may simply stop activities they don't like and pull out a toy they brought from home or doodle on their papers.

Parents of many first graders will grow weary of the word *fair*: It's not fair that they must go to school; it's not fair that they have homework; and it's not fair that they must take those long, boring tests.

Basic Test-Taking Strategies

Sometimes children score lower than they might on standardized tests because they approach testing in an inefficient and unproductive way. There are things that you can do

before the test—and that your child can do during the test—to make sure that he does as well as he can.

Before the Test

Be Patient. Perhaps the most effective strategy to use in preparing your child for standardized tests is patience. Remember that no matter how much pressure we put on children, they won't learn skills until they are neurologically, physically, cognitively, and emotionally ready to do so.

There's a delicate balance between challenging children to try difficult tasks they are ready for and pressuring them to perform tasks that are beyond their ability. Try to challenge your child, but if you see that he isn't making progress or he's getting frustrated, perhaps it's time to back off.

Be patient. Your child is just beginning a lifetime of learning. Normal children differ quite a bit in the speed at which they develop different skills. Many children whose parents thought they would never learn to read when they were in first grade become excellent readers later on. Realize too that you can't possibly be objective when it comes to your own child.

Talk with Your Child. Children at this age can have great insight into how they are doing in school. Your first grader may be able to tell you that he understands math but has trouble learning his vocabulary words. Remember too that problems with vision and hearing can surface at this age. Your child who passed vision and hearing screening last year may tell you that he can't see the chalkboard or that he can't hear the teacher this year.

Talk with Your Child's Teacher. It's amazing how many parents contact psychologists frantic to have their child evaluated for learning disabilities or emotional disturbance because of problems they think their child *might* be having in school, without ever speaking with the teacher about their concerns. Don't wait for an invitation or for problems to develop before you meet your child's teacher. Get to know the teacher as early in the school year as possible.

If your schedule permits, volunteer to help chaperone students during special programs or on field trips. Help bring refreshments on party days. Help your child's teacher to see you as an ally, someone he's comfortable contacting before small problems become big problems. Most teachers are eager to keep you updated on your child's progress, and they can give you materials and suggest activities for helping your child at home.

Don't Change the Routine. Many guides to standardized testing that schools send home to parents give mistaken advice about how to prepare children for a test, such as recommending that children go to bed early the night before or eat a high-protein breakfast on the morning of the test.

In fact, you should change as little as possible in your child's routine the day before and the morning of the test. If your child isn't used to going to bed at 8 p.m., then putting him to bed early the night before the test will only frustrate him and may actually make it more difficult for him to get to sleep by the normal time. If he is used to eating highly sugared cereal or just some buttered toast for breakfast, forcing him to eat a big breakfast will only make him feel sleepy or uncomfortable.

If you think an earlier bedtime is a good idea, make that change weeks before testing. If your child isn't eating a healthy breakfast, introduce better choices as far in advance as possible.

Neatness. Yes, neatness does count. Observe how neatly your child can fill in the bubbles, squares, and rectangles at the bottom of this page. If your child fills them in sloppily, overlaps the lines, erases a lot, or presses the pencil so hard that he gouges holes in the paper, you may want to have him practice fine-motor kinds of activities. If you have a computer, you can easily create sheets of capital *Os*, squares, and rectangles that your child can practice filling in. Have him color in coloring books and complete connect-the-dots pages.

Rewrite Math Problems. Sometimes children find it difficult to solve math problems when they are written in linear fashion. For example, consider the following problem:

$$19 - 3 = \_\_\_$$

Make sure you spend time practicing with your child now to solve all kinds of math problems, using a variety of math formats, before the standardized test.

Translate Word Problems to Math Problems. Sometimes students try to solve math word problems but have a difficult time translating the elements of the problems into mathematical expressions. For example, consider the following problem:

Samantha had 12 pennies. She gave her little brother 5 of them. How many did she have left?

If a student rewrote the problem as:

12 pennies
−5 pennies

he might solve it more readily. Spend time before standardized tests take place to work with your child on these skills.

Strategies During the Test

There are some strategies your child can use during standardized testing that have been shown to result in some degree of improvement in their scores. Talk about the strategies listed here with your child and remind him of them from time to time. Opportunities to practice with time for feedback and discussions are quite useful for young learners.

Bring Extra Pencils. Even if students are allowed to get up and sharpen pencils, the very act of getting up, sharpening the pencils, and returning to their seats will take away precious time that could be used answering several more questions. If your child breaks the point of a pencil and he only has to reach into his desk for another, he'll have more time to work on test questions.

Listen Carefully. It's astounding how many mistakes children make during testing because they simply don't listen to instructions or don't pay attention to demonstrations. Some children may circle the bubbles instead of filling them in; others don't put their names on the test answer sheets despite the fact that proctors guide them through this step. Still others begin marking their answers on the wrong side of the form or go to the wrong section to begin marking.

Mark the Bubble for the Correct Question. Many children simply make a mark without making sure they are marking the correct bubble. As a result, some answers have no bubbles marked, and others have two or more marked. At other times, a child may mark answer *D* when he meant to mark *C*. Convince your child that the machine used to scan the answer sheets won't be able to read minds, so he must make sure that the machine knows which marks to score by putting them in the correct bubbles.

Read the Entire Question before Answering. Many children simply begin wildly filling in bubbles without reading the entire question. The last few words in a question sometimes give the most important clues to the correct answer.

Read All Possible Answer Choices. Children tend to be impulsive. They may very well select the first plausible answer before reading a much better answer farther down the list.

Skip Difficult Items; Return to Them Later. Many children, especially perfectionists, will obsess about problems that cause them difficulty. They may spend so much time on these problems that they never get to problems that they would be able to answer correctly if they only had enough time left. On the first-grade level, many of the tests involve listening and therefore don't lend themselves to saving difficult items until later, but some do.

Refer to Pictures for Clues. Test publishers don't put random pictures in test booklets. The pictures may provide valuable clues that children can combine with what they already know to find correct answers.

The First Answer Isn't Always Best. One of the great myths of standardized testing is that you should stick with your first answer. In fact, research has found that students more often change incorrect answers to correct ones than the other way around. It's also possible for your child to improve his score by flagging answers he isn't sure about and returning to them after he completes the other items.

Use Context. Students can often find clues to correct answers by looking at descriptions, wording, and other information from the questions themselves.

Infer Word Meaning from Context. When we run across unfamiliar words, most of us rarely stop and run to the dictionary to look them up. Instead, we try to figure out the word's meaning in context. That is, we look for meaning in the other parts of a sentence or paragraph that gives us clues to what meanings would be appropriate. For example, consider this: "Johnny thought Maria was *gregarious*. She had so many friends that she never walked home alone." Even if we don't know the word *gregarious*, we can figure out some clues from the context, and we can figure out that the passage must be talking about something related to having friends.

Children can frequently figure out unfamiliar meanings from such clues.

Use Key Words. Look at the questions and try to determine the parts that are important to answering the question and those that aren't.

Watch for Absolute Words. Absolute words may be a clue that the answer using them is less likely to be correct. For example, an answer that says "Horses *always* live in suburban areas" is false, and the clue is the word *always*.

Eliminate Answer Choices. Sherlock Holmes was fond of saying, "Eliminate the impossible, and what remains is the truth." Children can often narrow down their choices among multiple-choice options by eliminating answers they know can't possibly be true. On practice tests, begin by allowing your child to actually cross out answers that can't possibly be true, and then ask him to start mentally eliminating answers. This practice is critical, because most standardized tests will not allow your child to mark his test booklet other than to indicate his final answer.

CHAPTER 2

Word Analysis

If a journey of a thousand miles begins with a single step, the first step in learning to read is *word analysis*. That may sound like an intimidating concept, but it's really just a fancy way of referring to the ability to recognize and decode individual printed words. Together with vocabulary development (see Chapter 3), word analysis skills allow a child to move on to independent reading.

In this chapter, you'll learn what a typical first grader should know about specific word analysis skills that most children will develop during first grade. We present suggested activities for helping your child strengthen word analysis skills, and some sample test questions similar to those that most typical first-grade standardized tests include.

What Your First Grader Should Be Learning

The alphabet is the cornerstone of word analysis, and most beginning first graders have learned to say the alphabet (although many still depend on the Alphabet Song to remember all the letters). Don't worry if your early first grader still has some problems saying the entire alphabet without the Alphabet Song, or if she runs letters together (such as saying "alimenopee" instead of the letters *L, M, N, O,* and *P*). This is quite common in the beginning of first grade. Many first graders also confuse letters, such as lowercase *b* and *d* or *q* and *p*.

Children should be able to easily recognize block uppercase letters when they enter first grade, although many do not know lowercase letters and most do not know letters in specialized fonts such as italics. By the end of first grade, children should be able to recite the alphabet automatically and reliably, distinguishing all individual letters in block upper- and lowercase as well as in common fonts such as italics, outline, and shadow.

How You Can Help Your Child

As you read through these chapters, you'll notice that you'll be able to use many of the suggested strategies to build and reinforce a wide range of different skills. This is because we don't develop skills in isolation; many learning skills develop together. For example, while a typical first grader develops her word-attack skills, she is simultaneously developing her vocabulary, spelling, reading recognition, and reading comprehension.

Read on to find some of the best ways to help your child boost her word analysis abilities in first grade.

Talk! The most effective way to ensure that your child learns word analysis skills is to talk to him. That may sound obvious, but in an age in which the typical father spends less than seven minutes a day with his children, it's worth stressing. Of course, we don't mean to pick on fathers here; in many modern American two-parent families, both parents work and neither has lots of free time to interact with children. In single-parent families, there may be even less time for parent–child interactions.

For example, after the end of the work and school day, it's quite common for one child to be doing homework in a bedroom, another to be surfing the Net on her computer in the den, one parent in the kitchen preparing dinner, another picking up the dirty socks in the living room or taking the dog for a walk. Dinnertime used to be the best time to connect, but today many families rarely sit down together to eat a meal at the same time: Soccer practice, babysitting, and late nights at work all disrupt the dinner hour.

That's why simply talking to your kids may seem simple but is actually often overlooked— and yet it's an extremely important way to boost language development. Talk to your kids. Talk about the weather, what she did today, what he saw on TV, what you bought at the store, what you saw on the way to the dentist, and so on. Note that this is also the best way to increase vocabulary. (See Chapter 3.)

Read Together. Another strategy for helping your first grader develop word analysis skills is to read to him. In fact, reading to your child is one of the more effective ways of helping him prepare to begin school and helping him to strengthen many other early academic skills.

If you're finding it hard to simply sit down and read a book with your child, make an appointment to do so, for at least 15 minutes a day. Thirty minutes or more is better. Most parents find that bedtime is a logical time to start, but any time will work. Turn off the TV, put the cell phone in message mode, set the pager on vibrate, and tell other family members to take care of themselves for awhile. This is reading time.

Read a variety of books, poems, and magazines. Let your child help select them. If you started reading to her when she was very young, don't stop. Some parents give up the nightly reading habit when their children enter first grade, but it will remain important for your child even as he gets older.

Follow the Words. When she was younger, your child probably enjoyed looking at the pictures as you read. Now that she is in first grade, point out the words that go with the pictures as she follows along.

For example, if there is a picture of Pete the Pirate, point out the words "Pete" and "pirate." As you read, run your finger along below the words. At first, your child will probably not take a great interest in the words, but over time, he will come to pay attention to the written text, and the association between the spoken and written words will become stronger.

Running your finger under the words as you read will also reinforce the fact that reading in English proceeds from left to right. (Many children, especially left-handers, will still try to read from right to left, so reinforcement of this skill is important.)

While you are reading, point out words, especially words that illustrate word analysis skills, such as contractions (*don't* or *won't*) or compound words (*backyard* or *background*).

Choose Good Books. At some point during first grade, your child should begin to develop an interest in reading on her own. Help her choose books at an appropriate early reading level, such as the *Dr. Seuss* books or the Little Golden Books. The *Dr. Seuss* books are especially good because of the rhyming patterns and repetitions of high-frequency words.

Let Kids Read to You. Have your first grader read to you, but be gentle in pointing out mistakes. First graders are still unsure about their reading skill and may be sensitive if you are overly critical.

If your child gets tired of reading out loud, try alternating: You read one page, then let your child read the next, and so on.

What to Expect with Today's Tests

Questions on standardized tests for first graders typically assess a number of skills, including:

- letter recognition
- beginning sounds
- ending sounds
- rhyming sounds

We discuss each of these areas and present a few sample questions to help your child understand and practice these skills.

Letter Recogniton

What Tests May Ask

First-grade standardized tests generally assess for firmly established letter-recognition skills. Questions often present model letters in upper-case block format, with possible answer choices in lowercase. This is an extra test of knowledge of lowercase letters.

Practice Skill: Letter Recognition

Directions: Choose the correct answers for the following questions.

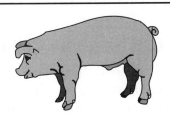

1 Here is a picture of a ⟍ ig. What is the <u>first</u> letter?

 Ⓐ d

 Ⓑ g

 Ⓒ b

 Ⓓ p

2 Here is a part of the alphabet: P Q R ___ T U V. Which letter is missing?

 Ⓐ j

 Ⓑ x

 Ⓒ s

 Ⓓ z

3 Which of these pairs of letters shows <u>different</u> letters?

 Ⓐ a A

 Ⓑ P q

 Ⓒ D d

 Ⓓ B b

(See page 111 for answer key.)

Beginning Sounds

Most school lesson plans for early readers emphasize beginning sounds first. Usually, this means that there is an emphasis on alphabet words, such as *A* is for *APPLE*, *B* is for *BOY*, and so on. Understanding beginning sounds will also require that your child be able to figure out *which* sound is actually the beginning sound.

What You and Your Child Can Do

Of course, as we discussed earlier, reading to your child is a wonderful way of stressing beginning sounds. Playing the "grandmother's house" game is a good way to work on a number of skills, including memory and beginning sounds. In this game, the first person chooses an object being with the letter A to take to grandmother's house; the second person must repeat the first item and add a second item beginning with the next letter in the alphabet, and so on:

You: "I went to grandmother's house and I took an Alligator..."

Child: "I went to grandmother's house and I took an Alligator and a Bear...

You: "I went to grandmother's house and I took an Alligator, a Bear, and a Candycane..."

What Tests May Ask

In assessing a child's understanding of beginning sounds, tests may ask questions that require the child to be able to recognize which sound of a word is the beginning sound. If she has problems with this type of task, encourage her to say the words aloud to determine which is the beginning sound.

Practice Skill: Beginning Sounds

Directions: Choose the correct answers for the following questions.

---

4 <u>C</u> is for <u>cat</u>. <u>D</u> is for <u>dog</u>. <u>E</u> is for <u>Emily</u>. <u>F</u> is for what?

Ⓐ fish

Ⓑ horse

Ⓒ rabbit

Ⓓ nose

---

5 Choose the word that <u>begins</u> with the same sound as the word in the picture:

Ⓐ table   Ⓑ rat

Ⓒ comb   Ⓓ dart

(See page 111 for answer key.)

Ending Sounds

Ending sounds tend to present more of a challenge than beginning sounds for early first graders. When asked to name ending sounds, many children name the beginning sounds instead. There is probably a developmental, neurological reason for this confusion. In any case, starting by about age 6, children will benefit from practice in this skill.

How You Can Help Your Child

If your child is having problems figuring out ending sounds, have him sound out the words and point out which sounds are the beginning sounds and which are the ending sounds.

What Tests May Ask

You can be sure that standardized tests will assess ending sounds—that is, how well your child can decipher the sounds at the ends of words. For first graders, the tests will probably include a range of easier items through more difficult questions. Questions will typically present several answers with somewhat similar ending sounds, with at least one choice using the same beginning sound as the ending sound the child needs to find.

Practice Skill: Ending Sounds

Directions: Choose the correct answers for the following questions.

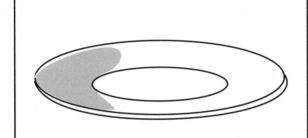

6 Here is a dish. Which word has the same <u>ending</u> sound as dish?

   Ⓐ ditch   Ⓑ foot

   Ⓒ show   Ⓓ crash

7 Which of these words has a different <u>ending</u> sound than the others?

   Ⓐ harm

   Ⓑ word

   Ⓒ worm

   Ⓓ swarm

(See page 111 for answer key.)

Rhyming Sounds

Younger children are thrilled at making their own rhymes. By first grade, most children are still playful enough to take great delight in continuing this game.

However, many first graders become quite confused by having different letters or letter combinations make the same sounds. For example, they often say that *bait* and *eight* rhyme when they hear them but insist that they don't rhyme when they see them written.

Children at this age tend to be inflexible when it comes to how they believe the rules of language should work. This would be fine in a language with predictable rules, but in English there are almost always exceptions. This is why English-speaking children often find pronunciations confusing. They have little patience with why *e*, for example, sometimes has the long *e* sound as in *free*, but at other times has a short *e* sound as in *pet*.

What You and Your Child Can Do

If your child mistakenly claims that words do or don't rhyme, have her sound out the words. But if she continues to make such mistakes, don't panic. Many children don't firmly grasp this skill until late second grade to early third grade.

Thinking up short rhymes should delight many children this age. Make a game of it: Begin a sentence and see if your child can think of some rhymes. Make it as silly as possible:

YOU START: The *cat* is wearing a...

CHILD: *Hat!*

YOU: While sitting on a...

CHILD: *Bat!*

YOU: ...and holding a...

CHILD: *Mat!*

If your child can't come up with a rhyme, you can supply one to keep the sentence going. This game can be played anywhere—in the car, sitting around the dinner table, or during bath time.

Here's a version of this game that takes more time, but has the added benefit of helping your child link printed rhymes with sounds: Get a stack of magazines and cut out lots of pictures of things that rhyme—bat, cat, mat, hat. Print the word on the picture. Try to get some rhyming words that aren't spelled the same (bait and state, for example). Spread them all out on a table, and have your child select a word to begin the nonsense sentence.

CHILD: The *bait* ...

YOU: ... is on the *gate* ...

(and so on).

What Tests May Ask

Expect standardized tests to assess rhyming sounds, using different letters and combinations making the same sound. Most tests will try to gauge your child's ability to recognize rhyming words. Tests will include questions in which all but the correct answer begin with the same letter; this may confuse children who are unsure of their ability to recognize rhymes. Questions may also include two words beginning with the same letter that sound the same, are spelled differently, yet both rhyme with the example word.

Practice Skill: Rhyming Sounds

Directions: Choose the correct answers for the following questions.

---

8 Which of these animal names rhymes with <u>fair</u>?

Ⓐ ferret

Ⓑ bear

Ⓒ fox

Ⓓ fish

---

9 Which of these words rhymes with <u>bait</u>?

Ⓐ great

Ⓑ ball

Ⓒ bit

Ⓓ bad

---

10 Find the word that doesn't rhyme with <u>plate</u>.

Ⓐ grate

Ⓑ great

Ⓒ plain

Ⓓ state

(See page 111 for answer key.)

Word Recognition and Sight Words

Beginning first graders are typically able to read and recite the alphabet, but their word recognition is generally limited to a few high-frequency words, such as pets' names or the words used to correspond to alphabet charts (such as *A* is for *Apple*). During first grade, most children begin to recognize many more words, as well as the number of pronunciation rules they internalize.

Children this age also become familiar with word families, such as those stating relationships, such as *higher*, *louder*, and *bigger*, in which—"-er" means more of something; or *friendliest*, *fastest*, and *prettiest*, in which "-est" means the *most* of something.

What You and Your Child Can Do

All the strategies we discussed at the beginning of the chapter work well here. Pointing to the text as you read to your child will allow her to follow along and recognize new words.

Play word games. Print simple words onto small index cards (including some you know your child hasn't learned yet) and put them into a hat. Have your child try to make simple sentences with the words.

Let your child play with a set of magnetized words on the refrigerator while you cook. Or buy a set of magnetized letters, and play word games on the fridge: You put some words together and see if she can recognize them.

Hands-on works well here. While you're at the grocery store, line up three apples of varying sizes. Ask your child, "Which apple is bigger? Which apple is the biggest?" At home, sort through your child's toys. "Which bear is smaller than that bear? Which bear is the smallest of all your bears?"

What Tests May Ask

Standardized tests are likely to assess what words your first grader can recognize, as well as the number of pronunciation rules she has internalized. Children make mistakes in this type of task when they fail to verbalize the sentence—softly and to themselves, if necessary—to check for how it sounds.

Practice Skill: Word Recognition and Sight Words

Directions: Choose the correct answers for the following questions.

---

11 Find the missing word in this sentence: Mary had to stay home today, but she said she would ___ to my house tomorrow.

   Ⓐ borrow   Ⓑ cover

   Ⓒ come   Ⓓ bring

---

12 Over means the same as:

   Ⓐ not under

   Ⓑ to the left of

   Ⓒ to the right of

   Ⓓ smaller than

---

13 Which of the words does NOT mean the <u>most</u> of something?

   Ⓐ highest   Ⓑ lower

   Ⓒ neatest   Ⓓ richest

(See page 111 for answer key.)

Vowel Sounds

The differentiation between vowel and consonant sounds will probably be foreign to beginning first graders and continue to pose great challenges as the year progresses. It's fairly common for even late first graders to be unable to label vowel versus consonant sounds, although by the end of the first year, many will be able to mimic the "oo" sound or to state that the letter *A* has both the short *A* sound as in "cat" and the long *A* as in "ate."

What You and Your Child Can Do

Play the "vowel sounds" game:

YOU: Can you think of a word in which the E says its name, like EEEven?

CHILD: Eat.

YOU: Eeyore.

CHILD: Each.

YOU: Now think of a word in which the O says its name, like Open.

CHILD: Over.

Or, play the rhyme game, stressing the vowel sounds.

YOU: I'm thinking of a word that rhymes with hoooot.

CHILD: BOOOt.

What Tests May Ask

Most commonly, first graders will be expected to answer questions about which pairs of words rhyme.

Practice Skill: Vowel Sounds

Directions: Choose the best answer.

---

14 Which two words rhyme?

Ⓐ boo, screw

Ⓑ ate, arm

Ⓒ him, tom

Ⓓ car, comb

---

15 What word rhymes with boot?

Ⓐ school   Ⓑ bun

Ⓒ both   Ⓓ hoot

(See page 111 for answer key.)

Word Study

Word study refers to the process of becoming familiar with the various rules for how we form and use words in the English language. This includes such assorted topics as how we combine two words to form one word (such as *side + walk = sidewalk*) and how we form contractions (such as *can + not = can't*).

Although early first graders will initially have some problems understanding such concepts, they will enjoy games in which they can detect the word combinations in compound words.

By the end of first grade, children should also have a much better command of the common contractions, such as *can't, don't, isn't,* and *wasn't.* But even then, most children will still have trouble with particularly difficult contractions, such as distinguishing *its* versus *it's.* (This is something some adults haven't mastered, so it's not surprising that it can be rough for first graders.)

What You and Your Child Can Do

Try some games to help your child figure out the compound word. For example, point out that the word *hotdog* is a combination of the words *hot* and *dog* and see if your child can compete with you to point out other words formed from two or more words, such as *toothpaste* and *headache.*

Give your child a magic marker and see how many contractions she can circle on the front page of a newspaper. Of course, there will be many words she doesn't know, but make this a sort of treasure hunt to be able to pick out contractions from the printed page.

If that seems too hard, have your child try to print a sentence with as many contractions as she can put in. Or you can compose a silly sentence filled with contractions and have her circle all of the contractions.

What Tests May Ask

Standardized tests typically assess word study by asking your child to detect compound words and contractions. The following questions are examples of the types of questions your child may encounter on a standardized test.

Practice Skill: Word Study

Directions: Choose the correct answers for the following questions.

16 Which word is made up of two <u>different</u> words?

ⓐ skateboard

ⓑ summer

ⓒ unhappy

ⓓ terrible

17 Which word is made up of two <u>different</u> words?

ⓐ unfair

ⓑ window

ⓒ suntan

ⓓ silly

18 <u>Can't</u> means the same as:

ⓐ does not care

ⓑ cannot

ⓒ do not

ⓓ was

19 <u>It's</u> means the same as:

ⓐ its

ⓑ its'

ⓒ it is

ⓓ it isn't

(See page 111 for answer key.)

CHAPTER 3

Vocabulary

A strong vocabulary is necessary for the development of good reading and writing skills. The areas of the brain that govern vocabulary are undergoing tremendous development by first grade—especially brain centers that control the speech we hear and understand, and the areas that control what we say to others.

There are two basic types of vocabulary your child needs to learn: Receptive vocabulary and expressive vocabulary. *Receptive vocabulary* refers to the words we recognize when we hear them or see them. For example, we may not use the word *tsunami* in our everyday language, but we recognize it when we hear the international news describe a tsunami that struck islands off the coast of Japan. Most people develop receptive vocabulary early: A preverbal child squeals with delight when we tell him that we're going to McDonald's for french fries. The child can't yet say "McDonald's" or "french fries," but he certainly understands these words. They are an example of receptive vocabulary.

Expressive vocabulary refers to the words we speak. For example, a young child might refer to her grandmother as "gandma"—that word becomes part of her expressive vocabulary. While she recognizes the word "grandmother" when her parents say, "Go give this to your grandmother," she refers to that individual as "gandma." In this case, "grandmother" is part of her receptive vocabulary, while "gandma" is part of her expressive vocabulary.

What Your First Grader Should Be Learning

By the time children are in first grade, they've begun to realize that there is a world outside of themselves. Typical first graders have oral vocabularies of 2,500 words or more, but they're still "magical" and subjective in their thinking. This means they can't deal very well with many abstract concepts, especially those that relate to time. Don't be surprised if your child's receptive vocabulary (the words he recognizes) is far greater than his expressive vocabulary (the words he says).

How You Can Help Your Child

There are many different ways to help your child enrich his vocabulary (and also develop a wide range of other skills needed during first grade).

Reading

By now, you've probably gotten the message that reading to your children is one of the best ways to help them strengthen many academic areas. Early first graders still enjoy having someone read to them, and even late first graders enjoy being read to (although some may need a little coaxing).

Read a wide variety of materials to your children. If she has a new hamster, find elementary books on hamsters or stories featuring hamsters. If there's a new baby on the way, find books with characters expecting a new sibling.

Your local librarian can be your best friend in helping you find books on a wide variety of subjects at a level appropriate for your first grader. Children's interest in subject matter can be a real motivator for them to struggle through books even beyond their reading level, and the exposure to the new vocabulary in those books will increase both their receptive and expressive vocabularies.

Hobbies

By the time children are in the first grade, many are beginning to have hobbies that present another opportunity to boost their vocabularies. If Melissa enjoys putting together models of ships, look up ship terms such as "port," "starboard," "keel," "mast," and so on. If Jeff enjoys his new computer, become familiar with computers yourself and help him learn terms, such as "RAM" and "modem."

Children are often fascinated by their parents' hobbies and will eagerly become involved with them. For example, if Mom is working toward her Black Belt in karate, her child will probably be fascinated by learning the names of the forms, kicks, and punches. If Dad enjoys collecting coins, a first grader will eagerly help go through rolls of coins he brings home from the bank or help him catalog his collection and learn terms along the way.

Travel

Going places and seeing new things is a powerful way to increase your first grader's vocabulary. After a trip to the beach, children might come back with such words as "barnacle," "tide," or "sand dollar."

Talk and Listen

Almost all of us get too busy sometimes to talk with or listen to our children often enough. It's easy to get caught up in our own worlds, with our pressures and worries, and many parents aren't aware how powerful simply talking and listening can be when it comes to boosting a child's knowledge of the world.

Children whose parents speak to and listen to them have much richer expressive and receptive vocabularies than those whose parents don't. First graders are generally thrilled to talk to the older people in their lives. They enjoy hearing Grandma talk about how she stood on a wooden box and stirred the syrup as a child while her family processed sugar cane, and they come home with new words like "blackstrap." They'll be fascinated to hear Grandpa talk about growing up during the Depression, when the mill shut down and the family couldn't afford shoes. They'll love to hear about what life was like before computers, video games, and even electric lights, learning vocabulary such as "oil lamps," "lard," and "outhouse."

Television

There is certainly enough evidence that children today spend more time watching TV than they spend on their homework and physical fitness activities combined. But used appropriately, TV can increase a child's exposure to the world and boost vocabulary.

Sesame Street is still very effectively teaching children letters and new words. There is a substantial body of research indicating that children who watch the program begin school much better prepared for it than those who don't.

Word Games

Word games can be real vocabulary boosters for your child. Here's an old-fashioned game that's still a favorite: One child puts on a hat with a hat band (such as Grandpa's old field hat). Print words on index cards with different nouns, such as "cow" or "fire truck," and put one card at a time in the hat band so that everyone but the child wearing the hat can see the word. The others take turns giving one clue at a time, until the child guesses the word.

Even first graders can enjoy a simplified version of Charades, guessing their favorite TV shows and movies, songs and books. Or try "Thumper." Players sit around a table thumping the tabletop in time; the first child calls out the name of a category, such as "games with balls." Then the children go around the table and call out something from that category, such as "baseball" before a prearranged number of thumps has passed. The first player who can't name an item from the category (or who calls out a name that someone else already called out) must leave the table. The final player left at the table wins.

Commercial games are good sources of vocabulary development for first graders. Games such as *Concentration, Pyramid,* and *Password* have been around for years and can help boost vocabulary (although some may need to be simplified for a first grader's ability). Children's versions of *Scrabble* provide a great way to teach spelling and vocabulary.

Catalogs

Very young children enjoy looking at the pictures in catalogs, and even first graders enjoy going through them. Try cutting out catalog pictures and pasting them onto index cards to make flash cards. The more exotic the catalog, the better.

Writing

First graders love to dictate stories and have you write them down; or let your child dictate stories into a tape recorder. He'll enjoy having you write down or type the stories so he can read them. Most first graders will usually dictate more complex stories with larger vocabularies than they can actually read by themselves. Because they were the authors, they will be able to identify many of the unfamiliar words from the context.

If your child really enjoys this activity, buy a "book making" kit designed to allow your child to create a story, draw pictures to go along with the words, and mail in the kit; in about two weeks, he'll receive a hardcover printed copy of the book for about the price of a video.

Dictionaries/Encyclopedias

First grade is a good time for kids to learn how to look up unfamiliar words. There are many dictionaries appropriate for first grade, but there will be times when your child will need to use a more advanced dictionary. For example, suppose your child hears the word *marsupials*, he probably won't find that word in a children's dictionary. He may hear *Bill Nye The Science Guy* talk about deep space objects on TV, and want to know more; he will need to look up the word or phrase in an encyclopedia. Encourage the habit of consulting dictionaries and encyclopedias.

Model the behavior you want to teach: Make sure your child sees *you* using a dictionary. If you're reading *Jack and the Beanstalk* and you get to the part where Jack asks for "five pounds" when he sells the cow, many first graders will ask: "What's a pound?" If you don't know how much a British pound sterling is worth, go look it up in an almanac or dictionary, or consult the newspaper for the latest bank rates.

The Internet

The Internet is rapidly becoming a wonderful resource for kids to look up anything they don't know. With proper supervision and careful thought, the Internet can be a very effective search tool.

For example, Betsy came across the word *aglet* while reading about a favorite tennis player's foot injury that was somehow caused by her shoes. A search of her first-grade dictionary revealed nothing, and a search of the large family dictionary was unsuccessful. Only when Betsy and her dad searched the Internet did they learn that *aglet* (French for "needle") refers to the hard tip on a shoestring. Child-friendly Internet search engines include:

- http://www.yahooligans.com
- http://www.familyplanet.com
- http://www.altavista.com
- http://www.excite.com

Meta-search engines combine several different search engines for a very intensive search. Some of these engines are:

- http://www.dogpile.com
- http://www.askjeeves.com
- http://www.mamma.com
- http://www.savvysearch.com
- http://www.metacrawler.com

Picture Vocabulary

Picture vocabulary refers to the words we recognize when we see illustrations of them. The ability to *name* objects in a picture is called expressive picture vocabulary; the ability to *recognize* objects in a picture is called receptive picture vocabulary.

Picture vocabulary development is important in learning how to read. When you read to your child, he learns to associate pictures with the words he hears you read. That skill eventually leads to the ability to read words without pictures.

For example, when a picture book for young children illustrates a picture of an apple with the word "apple" under the picture, a child eventually comes to associate the written word with the picture; later on, he can recognize that the written word "apple" refers to that piece of fruit. Adults unfamiliar with kindergarten and first-grade classrooms may be amused to find that the teacher has put labels on the different objects around the room, such as "window," "door," "hamster," and so on.

Early first graders should be accustomed to learning new words by associating them with pictures. Remember that many kindergarten teachers emphasize teaching colors by showing children cards with colors on them and having children name the colors. Unlike kindergarteners who rely on naming pictures they see, first graders are typically able to begin learning to associate the pictures not only with the sound but also with the words in written form.

When it comes to picture vocabulary, it's important that children begin forming receptive picture vocabulary before they begin forming expressive picture vocabulary. As they grow older, they will have a larger receptive than expressive picture vocabulary.

What You and Your Child Can Do

To develop picture vocabulary, get out the family photo album. Kids love looking at photos, *especially* pictures of themselves. As you turn the page, ask your first grader a series of questions:

- Which picture shows you learning to skate?
- What are you doing in this picture?

For more advanced fun, write a series of verbs on index cards (skating, swimming, sleeping, running, crying, eating). Now go back to that family album. Point to a photo, hold up three or four cards and ask your child to select the card that matches what she's doing in the photo.

What Tests May Ask

Standardized tests in first grade gauge a child's ability to either name objects (expressive picture vocabulary) or recognize objects (receptive picture vocabulary) that he sees in pictures. For example, a test question assessing expressive picture vocabulary might ask a child to look at a picture and then choose the word that correctly describes what the subject of the picture is doing.

To assess receptive picture vocabulary, the test might ask a child to read a word or listen to a word read aloud by the teacher (such as "running") and then choose one picture out of a group of pictures that represents the word "running." This requires the child to retrieve from memory the label for what the picture shows.

Practice Skill: Picture Vocabulary

Directions: Choose the correct answers for the following questions.

1 Which of these words tells what the children are doing?

Ⓐ sharing

Ⓑ fighting

Ⓒ crying

Ⓓ eating

2 Which word tells what the dog is doing?

Ⓐ running

Ⓑ barking

Ⓒ sleeping

Ⓓ eating

3 Which picture shows the children <u>sharing</u>?

Ⓐ

Ⓑ

Ⓒ

Ⓓ

4 Which picture shows the cat <u>eating</u>?

Ⓐ  Ⓑ

Ⓒ

Ⓓ

(See page 111 for answer key.)

Word Reading

Word reading is the same thing as *sight vocabulary*; both refer to the words children can name when they see them in print. Although early first graders are typically able to recognize a few pertinent words, such as their names or well-known words or phrases such as *Toys R Us*, their recognition repertoire will vastly increase during first grade. Most children this age increase their word reading ability to include many one- and two-syllable words and even a few three-syllable words. The words they learn typically refer to concrete concepts.

What You and Your Child Can Do

Playing common word games can be very effective in helping with sight vocabulary. If you want to build your child's vocabulary, try printing a number of nouns found around your home on index cards. Attach tape to each card and, one by one, ask your child to read the word and then stick the word to the correct object around the home.

As the child becomes better able to read these words, try adding some excitement: How many items can the child label in 60 seconds? 20 seconds? 10 seconds?

Playing "treasure hunt" can be a good way to boost vocabulary. Give your child a list of items to find, including some words that may be a bit of a challenge. You can start with nouns ("apple," "book," "hat") and then branch out into adjectives ("yellow apple," "large book," "hard hat").

What Tests May Ask

Curriculum standards of most schools and states place the most emphasis on developing word reading in first grade, so this is something you'll certainly find on standardized tests. The following sample questions are typical of items your child may encounter.

Practice Skill: Word Reading

Directions: Choose the correct answers for the following questions.

5 What word goes with this picture?

  Ⓐ tomorrow   Ⓑ selfish

  Ⓒ polite   Ⓓ unhappy

6 Which of these words means "baby dog"?

  Ⓐ doggy   Ⓑ scrod

  Ⓒ baby   Ⓓ puppy

7 Look at the picture above. Here are a mother, father, son, and daughter. Together, they make what?

  Ⓐ family   Ⓑ litter

  Ⓒ tribe   Ⓓ herd

---

8 Which of these words means "glad"?

Ⓐ crying ⒷⒷ happy

Ⓒ weekend ⒹⒹ rude

(See page 111 for answer key.)

CHILD: (choosing the word "pig"): It's an animal with four feet.

PLAYER ONE: Horse!

CHILD: No. It's an animal with four feet and pink skin.

PLAYER: Mouse!

CHILD: No. It's an animal with four feet, pink skin, and a curly tail.

PLAYER: Pig!

Word Meaning

You may remember from your school days that it's much easier to *understand* a foreign language than it is to *speak* it. Your children have this same experience when they learn to speak and read their native tongue. Children often understand what they want before they can verbalize specific words for it. By the time your child begins first grade, he should be able to at least describe in detail what he wants, even if he can't name the precise word. For example, if Sam doesn't know that we call a certain object a "compass" but he needs one to draw a circle, he can at least ask his father, "Where is that thing that I put my pencil in and it draws circles?"

Early first graders may not understand the concept of definitions, however. When someone asks him to give a definition of *horse*, for example, T. J. may respond, "It's a horse." But by the end of first grade, he should be able to begin to offer simple dictionary-type definitions for common words, such as, "A horse is an animal that you ride."

What You and Your Child Can Do

Play "definitions," a sort of reverse 20 Questions. This works well for a family or group of several children. One person chooses a simple word (such as "dog" or "cat") and then must describe it to the others.

What Tests May Ask

Standardized tests at the first-grade level typically assess the child's ability to define words in two ways: by giving a definition and then asking the child to select the correct word; and by giving a word and asking the child to match it up with the correct definition.

Practice Skill: Word Meaning

Directions: Choose the correct answers for the following questions.

---

9 Which of these words means "to let someone else use your things"?

Ⓐ borrow ⒷⒷ pay

ⒸⒸ share ⒹⒹ trap

---

10 Which of these words means "to remove dirt"?

Ⓐ jump ⒷⒷ iron

Ⓒ wash ⒹⒹ wear

---

11 Which of these words means "to buy something"?

Ⓐ play

Ⓑ pay

Ⓒ wash

Ⓓ jump

12 Which of the definitions goes with the word <u>draw</u>?

Ⓐ Put something dirty into the sink and clean it with soap and water.

Ⓑ Make a statue of a person out of clay.

Ⓒ Take a picture of something with a camera.

Ⓓ Make a picture of something with a pencil and paper.

13 Which of the definitions goes with the word <u>wade</u>?

Ⓐ Get clothes clean by putting them in soap and water.

Ⓑ Make a tasty dessert by adding milk to pudding mix.

Ⓒ Make a dress by using a needle and thread.

Ⓓ Cross a stream by walking through water.

14 Which of the definitions goes with the word <u>automobile</u>?

Ⓐ animal with whiskers and a tail

Ⓑ object that has four tires and goes on the road

Ⓒ object with bars at a zoo

Ⓓ something good to eat

15 Maria said, "I need to draw a straight line. May I borrow your ___?"

Ⓐ ruler

Ⓑ ribbon

Ⓒ rubber band

Ⓓ glass

(See page 111 for answer key.)

Synonyms

Synonyms are words that sound different but mean the same thing, such as "car" and "automobile." Most early first graders and almost all late first graders understand the concept that two different words can mean the same thing. In fact, many first graders enjoy games in which they come up with many words for the same concept. Your first grader's repertoire of synonyms will focus on simple synonyms, emphasizing concrete similarities.

What You and Your Child Can Do

Word games featuring synonyms can be lots of fun to play with your first grader. Try a challenge test: How many synonyms can your child come up with for a word?

YOU: House.

CHILD: Home, mansion, cabin, cottage.

What Tests May Ask

Typically, standardized tests include at least a few questions asking your child about words that mean the same thing but that may be spelled differently. The tests present pairs of words and ask the first grader to choose which pair means the same thing.

Practice Skill: Synonyms

Directions: Choose the correct answers for the following questions.

16 Which pair of words means the same?

Ⓐ mood   moon

Ⓑ sam   same

Ⓒ car   automobile

Ⓓ train   bus

17 Which pair of words does NOT mean the same?

Ⓐ fix   break

Ⓑ boat   ship

Ⓒ hurry   rush

Ⓓ middle   center

18 Find the word that means the same as the underlined word in this sentence: Jerry had to <u>hit</u> the nail very hard to make it go into the board.

Ⓐ tool

Ⓑ board

Ⓒ crack

Ⓓ strike

(See page 111 for answer key.)

Antonyms

Antonyms are words that have opposite meanings, such as "up" and "down." Most first graders are fascinated by opposites, and they enjoy games in which they must identify antonyms. As with synonyms, your first grader's repertoire will be basic and will emphasize common opposite pairs.

What You and Your Child Can Do

Try this car game: You name one word, and have your child name its opposite. You can start with simple one-word antonyms and progress to more complicated ones. For example, if you point to the pasture you're passing and say: "Black cow lying down," your child would then say, "White bull standing up."

What Tests May Ask

Typically, standardized tests include at least a few questions asking your child about words that mean the opposite. The tests present a word and then ask the first grader to choose which word is its opposite. The tests may ask the child to choose among words that sound the same or have the same beginning sounds to ensure the child really knows the opposite.

Practice Skill: Antonyms

Directions: Find the word that means the *opposite* of the underlined word in the following sentences.

---

19 Jerry put on a <u>white</u> hat.

  (A) cowboy

  (B) black

  (C) green

  (d) yellow

---

20 We liked the movie, but it was too <u>long</u>.

  (A) heavy

  (B) black

  (C) short

  (D) easy

---

21 The dog was lying on a <u>soft</u> bed.

  (A) hard

  (B) green

  (C) large

  (D) smooth

---

22 Susan always cried when she was <u>sad</u>.

  (A) tall

  (B) tired

  (C) happy

  (D) seven

(See page 111 for answer key.)

Words in Context

As first graders become more competent readers, they become better at predicting words. This is an element of reading comprehension that helps children learn to proofread and understand the meaning of written passages.

Almost all first graders read words in robotic fashion at first, oblivious to the relationship among the words. In reading, the words should come together to create a whole. As first graders become better able to recognize written words, they become more comfortable with perceiving the sentence in its entirety.

At the same time, they should become better at predicting words and spotting when a word is missing or when the wrong one has been used. For example, in the sentence: "Lisa got on her bike and rode green Grandmother's house," some first graders will simply read the words without catching the erroneous use of the word *green*.

What Tests May Ask

Most standardized tests assess how well first graders understand the relationships among words in a sentence by presenting sentences with blanks that need to be filled in, or by asking the child to find the word that doesn't belong.

Practice Skill: Words in Context

Direction: Choose the word that should go in the blank for the following sentences.

---

23 Tommy's mother said, "Tommy, your dog has been in the house all day. You need to take Baxter for a _____."

  (A) feed   (B) dog

  (C) walk   (D) cat

---

24 Lisa's parents gave her a new bike for her _____.

Ⓐ birthday

Ⓑ yesterday

Ⓒ bicycle

Ⓓ happy

25 The cat ran after the _____.

Ⓐ tree

Ⓑ giggle

Ⓒ mouse

Ⓓ walk

Directions: Find the word that doesn't belong in the following sentences.

26 Susan's dog ran purple the store.

Ⓐ ran

Ⓑ purple

Ⓒ store

Ⓓ Susan

27 Sam's mother bought orange a toy.

Ⓐ bought

Ⓑ mother

Ⓒ orange

Ⓓ toy

(See page 111 for answer key.)

CHAPTER 4

Reading Comprehension

Learning how to read individual words is certainly important, but just as important is learning to make sense of what we read. Reading to understand, known as reading comprehension, is a higher-order academic skill that many children won't develop to any great degree until they are older.

Many first-grade curricula emphasize the development of reading comprehension only superficially, because other skills usually come first. Word recognition, recognition of words in context, and the ability to make inferences from reading are still undergoing basic development. Nevertheless, there are some important skills required for reading comprehension that children are developing during first grade:

- listening comprehension,
- picture comprehension,
- sentence comprehension, and
- story comprehension.

Keep in mind, however, that your first grader may well find her reading comprehension slowed down by the relatively small number of words she can recognize. She'll benefit from attempts to increase her word recognition, as we emphasized in Chapter 3. Continued emphasis on the development of word recognition and looking words up in the dictionary will increase her ability to understand what she reads.

What Your First Grader Should Be Learning

By the time they reach first grade, most children are able to intelligently infer and anticipate from what is read to them. For example, if you're reading *The Legend of Sleepy Hollow* and stop as the Headless Horseman chases Ichabod Crane toward the bridge and ask: "What do you think will happen next?" very young children might come up with something such as: "He'll turn on his power shield and get away."

Even early first graders should be able to make more appropriate predictions, such as, "The Headless Horseman kills him," or "He gets over the bridge so the Headless Horseman can't get him."

How You Can Help Your Child

If you've read to your child (especially from a very young age), by the time she begins first grade she should be able to follow story lines, understand the facts as they unfold, predict outcomes, and make inferences. Reading to your children is a sound way of preparing them for reading comprehension.

Here are some other ways you can improve all types of reading comprehension, including listening comprehension, picture comprehension, sentence comprehension, and story comprehension.

Review. As you read to first graders, you should begin to look for more complex stories than your child can read herself. At appropriate times, stop and ask your child what has happened. Here's an example:

The pirate was so happy as he dug that he could not stand to wait until he found the treasure. He hit something hard. He saw a box. He pulled the box out of the hole and opened it. His eyes grew sad when he saw what was inside.

After you read this paragraph, you could stop and ask: "Do you think there was a treasure in the box?" This requires the child to make an inference from the facts.

"No? Well, what do you think was in the box?" This requires your child to make a prediction of what will happen next based on the facts and an inference.

Predict. Start to use prediction strategies with your child. Before you read a new story to your child, flip through the book and:

- Look at pictures.
- Read titles.
- Get a feel for the length and the subject.
- Read any blurbs on the jacket.

Then ask: "What do you think this story is about?" Discuss your child's predictions, and offer some of your own. Then read the story, noting when what actually happens agrees with or disagrees with what you predicted. Ask your child to tell you the story, and go back and double-check the passages that you or your child can't recall.

Have Your Child Read. By the end of first grade, your child will begin to enjoy reading to you. Choose age-appropriate readers such as the *Berenstain Bears* and *Dr. Seuss* books that your child will be able to read out loud with little or no help.

You also can resurrect books that you read to your child when she was younger; she can now read them to you. This is tremendously exciting to most first graders! Although the stories in many of these resurrected books are rather easy for first graders and would not hold their interest if you were reading the books to them, many kids this age will be very proud that they can read these books to their parents, or even to a younger brother or sister.

Because your child will already be familiar with the story lines in these books, she will be better able to figure out words she doesn't recognize.

Stock the Library. Whether you're looking for books to read to children or for those children can read for themselves, a well-stocked children's library can be a blessing. Many churches, synagogues, community centers, day care centers, and preschools have ample materials on a level appropriate for first graders. Bookstores and large book chains hold regular story times for children of different ages.

These places can give you and your children opportunities to preview books to make sure that they're age-appropriate, that your child will like them, and that the content is appropriate.

BOOK SUGGESTIONS

There are many books available for children of first-grade age, such as *Tom Sawyer* and the *Hardy Boys* or *Nancy Drew* mysteries, which may be too difficult for children to read themselves, but which they can understand. Again, a children's librarian or your child's teacher can recommend books appropriate for your child. Mysteries and adventures are particularly good at encouraging children to begin anticipating and predicting. Even books as challenging as *Lord of the Rings* may interest a first grader when read out loud by a parent.

Listening Comprehension

Before children can understand what they read, they must be able to follow a story line, a skill they develop by hearing what others tell them. (A more comprehensive discussion of listening appears in Chapter 5.) Parents who read to their children note that very early in their lives, toddlers enjoy being read to even though they don't always understand the words. Parents have reported that toddlers seemed perfectly happy even being read to from catalogs or cookbooks! That's because very young children seem to take comfort more in the sound of a parent's voice, with a certain tone and volume, than in the ability to comprehend in detail what the story says.

As children mature, they begin to appreciate and anticipate a story line, and begin to make predictions. As they begin to read on their own, they build on those skills.

First-grade teachers often pause during a story and ask students what they think will happen next. Early first graders are usually able to make intelligent predictions.

What Tests May Ask

Typically, standardized tests for first graders provide part of a story, and then ask students to predict what will happen next.

Practice Skill: Listening Comprehension

Directions: Say the following: "I am going to read you part of a story. I will ask you to tell me what you think will happen next."

Read the following: All of Devon's friends sat around the table and watched as Devon blew out the candles on the cake. Then they all sang a song.

1 What song do you think they sang?

Ⓐ "The Itsy Bitsy Spider"

Ⓑ "Happy New Year"

Ⓒ "The Alphabet Song"

Ⓓ "Happy Birthday to You"

Directions: Read the following:

Maria was so sad. She could not find the necklace her grandmother had sent her. Suddenly, she smiled. She ran to her room and opened her jewelry box on her dresser. She said, "I thought so!"

2 What do you think she found inside?

Ⓐ a pretty ring she could wear instead

Ⓑ her necklace

Ⓒ a silver dollar

Ⓓ a picture of her grandmother

Directions: Read the following:

Baxter, Biscuit, and Sparky ran barking after Boots. Boots ran up the tree and hissed and meowed at them until Baxter, Biscuit, and Sparky decided to go chase a car down the street.

3 What are Baxter, Biscuit, and Sparky?

Ⓐ squirrels

Ⓑ cats

Ⓒ dogs

Ⓓ cars

4 In the same story, what is Boots?

Ⓐ a squirrel

Ⓑ a cat

Ⓒ a dog

Ⓓ a car

(See page 111 for answer key.)

Picture Comprehension

By early first grade, children should be able to look at a complex picture and draw inferences from clues it contains. For example, when a first grader sees a photo of John F. Kennedy, Jr. saluting as his father's casket goes by, even children who are unfamiliar with the assassination and who have never seen the photograph before should be able to infer that the little boy in the picture is showing his respect. They might say something such as: "He's saluting because the soldiers are marching by" or "Everybody's sad because someone died." The ability to draw inferences from pictures is another skill that children will later build on to be able to draw inferences from what they read.

What Tests May Ask

Standardized tests assess picture comprehension by presenting a drawing, photo, or cartoon and asking the child to answer a question based on the picture. Some questions may require the child to look at the picture and infer what is happening from clues in the picture.

Practice Skill: Picture Comprehension

Directions: Look at the following pictures and answer the questions.

5 Why are the children sad?

Ⓐ One of them broke the window.

Ⓑ They are playing ball.

Ⓒ It is really football season.

Ⓓ They lost their ball.

6 What do you think the people are watching?

Ⓐ a rocket launch

Ⓑ a ball game

Ⓒ a movie

Ⓓ a car race

(See page 111 for answer key.)

Sentence Comprehension

Because early first graders continue to struggle with word recognition, they are usually able to understand only sentences with simple, concrete words used in a standard way. For example, an early first grader would understand sentences such as "Carol wears a blue shirt," or "The brown dog is running." By the end of first grade, children should begin to understand sentences that require some early abstract reasoning, such as "Kara is sharing the kitten with her sister," or "Leslie is angry at Shirley."

What Tests May Ask

Typical standardized questions assessing sentence comprehension in first grade usually present a sentence and then ask students to answer a question about the sentence.

Practice Skill: Sentence Comprehension

Directions: Read the sentences below and decide which word or picture goes with the sentence.

7 If you cut your finger, put on one of these.

 Ⓐ knife   Ⓑ band-aid

 Ⓒ fish hook   Ⓓ doctor

8 If you want to take a bath, reach for this.

 Ⓐ car   Ⓑ dog

 Ⓒ soap   Ⓓ book

9 Bill is glad to see John.

10 Suzy is boxing with her friend Sally.

Story Comprehension

Because they are not skilled at comprehending written words, first graders typically understand only very primitive stories that they read. Although they begin to recognize more complex and abstract words by the end of first grade, their command of such words is so erratic that they are still limited in story comprehension.

What Tests May Ask

Books at the first-grade level typically help children understand stories by including many pictures that give clues to the stories. Although many books for this age include pictures, standardized test questions make it clear in instructions that children can't answer test questions only by looking at the pictures. In these tests, some of the questions require children to recount simple facts. Others expect a child not only to understand the facts but to draw inferences from them.

Practice Skill: Story Comprehension

Directions: Read the story and then answer the questions. The picture will NOT tell you the answers to the questions.

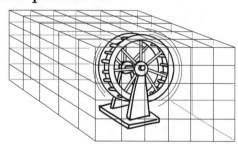

Story: My name is Buffy. I live in a nice cage and have lots of food and water. I like to run in my wheel all night while my boy Ross sleeps. Ross likes to get me out and pet me and tell me how pretty I am and what soft fur I have. I like it when he feeds me peanuts.

11 What am I?

Ⓐ

Ⓑ

Ⓒ   Ⓓ

Story: Shannon keeps her horse Daisy at her grandmother's farm. Grandmother called Shannon to tell her that Daisy had just had a colt. Shannon ran squealing to her mother and asked her if she could go to Grandmother's farm.

12 Who is Daisy?

Ⓐ Shannon's grandmother

Ⓑ Shannon's mother

Ⓒ Shannon's colt

Ⓓ Shannon's horse

13 Who called Shannon?

- Ⓐ Shannon's grandmother
- Ⓑ Shannon's mother
- Ⓒ Shannon's colt
- Ⓓ Shannon's horse

14 Why did she call Shannon?

- Ⓐ to tell Shannon that she was coming to Shannon's house for a visit
- Ⓑ to tell Shannon that her horse had a colt
- Ⓒ to talk to Shannon's mother
- Ⓓ to see if Shannon wanted to come live with her

15 Why was Shannon squealing?

- Ⓐ She dropped the phone on her foot.
- Ⓑ She was happy.
- Ⓒ She was sad.
- Ⓓ She did not want to talk to Grandmother.

(See page 111 for answer key.)

CHAPTER 5

Listening

In the past, standardized tests tended to emphasize reading and math, largely ignoring the rich array of other skills children develop in school.

Today, most standardized tests include at least some questions designed to assess how well a child listens. This is important because youngsters who have problems listening (whether because of hearing loss, a learning disability, or poor listening habits) will have problems learning in school.

Detailed discussions of hearing problems and learning disabilities are beyond the scope of this book. Instead, in this chapter we focus on helping children learn to listen who have the physical ability to hear and the learning processes necessary to understand what they hear.

What Your First Grader Should Be Learning

Listening and language skills are both very important in first grade. By the time they enter first grade, most children have begun to be able to control the internal factors that govern their ability to listen much better than they could as younger children.

By the time they enter first grade, most children are able to discriminate what spoken information is important and what isn't. They are still developing *sustained listening*—the ability to listen for very long periods. Most first graders should be able to look at the person doing the

speaking and begin asking pertinent questions to further their understanding.

Language skills are also important in listening. Although we don't expect first graders to be able to correctly label nouns, verbs, adjectives, and adverbs, almost all youngsters this age understand the difference between the *action*, who *performed* the action, and *to whom or what* the action was performed. They also understand possession, such as when we say, "Susie's cat" or "Danny's pencil."

Most English-speaking first graders understand that in most sentences, who or what comes first, the action comes next, and the person or thing acted on comes last. When we say: "Tina's brown dog is running down the long road," we understand that *brown* describes the dog, not Tina; and *long* describes the road.

Even early first graders should have mastered the basic skills used in the English language to communicate common, concrete ideas. Although we wouldn't expect them to understand a line from Shakespeare's *As You Like It*, we do expect them to understand simple direct sentences.

How You Can Help Your Child

If you want your first grader to be a good listener, you've got to give him something to listen to. By now it should come as no surprise that reading to your children is the best way to boost their listening skills.

Hearing ideas being expressed in standard ways helps children learn to recognize the correct form in which they will receive information. That, in turn, helps them learn how to extract information from what they hear. Here are some terrific ways to boost your child's listening ability.

Read Interesting Books. If you read books to your child that he's interested in, he'll learn to pay attention for long periods of time; this is called sustained listening. Get your children to help seek out interesting books and stories.

Read with Expression. As you read to your children, ham it up: Read the stories with feeling and speak the dialog using the tones and inflections that you think the characters would use if they were standing in front of you. This will help maintain a child's attention and help him learn to better anticipate the flow of what he hears.

Ask Questions Often. As you read to your child, stop occasionally and ask pertinent questions to make sure he's listening, such as: "Boy! What do you think about that?" Encourage him to listen actively by asking him to predict what will happen next, how he thinks the characters feel, and what he would do in a similar situation. For example, when you read that Little John knocked Robin Hood off the bridge and Robin was lying in the mud, ask: "How do you think Robin Hood felt about that?"

Look It Up! Encourage your child to speak up when you read something that he doesn't understand. If there's a word he doesn't know, help him learn how to look it up in a dictionary. Model the behavior you want by telling your child when you don't understand something. For example, if the passage says: "Paul was sanguine about Emily's suggestion," and you aren't sure what "sanguine" means, say so. Let your child see you go to the dictionary and look it up.

Communicate. Make sure that you talk to your children. When you're driving in the car, turn down the radio and chat. During dinner, switch off the TV and talk. It really doesn't matter what the subject is—just talk.

Model Good Listening. Show what it means to engage in sustained listening by listening and acknowledging what your child says. Of course, if you're driving, you can't maintain eye contact, but you can acknowledge that you're paying attention by making statements such as "Uh-huh," or "She did?"

Model active listening by asking pertinent questions, such as: "What is she angry at Judy about? I thought she and Judy were best friends," or, "How do you feel about that?"

Play a Game. Games can provide an excellent opportunity for children to brush up on their listening skills. In a group, the old party game "Gossip" or "Whisper Down the Lane" can make listening fun. In this game, the first person silently reads a sentence from a card, such as: "The boy's ears were so big his head looked like a car with the doors open." He then repeats it to the second child, who whispers the message to the third child, and so on. The final child in the circle then announces the message, which frequently bears little resemblance to the original message.

The "picnic" game is another good way to boost listening skills. Each child chooses an item to take to a picnic, starting with an item that begins with the first letter of the alphabet. The next child must repeat that item and then add an item beginning with the second letter of the alphabet. To do well in this game, the child must pay close attention to what each person says:

CHILD 1: I'm going on a picnic and I'm taking an ant.

CHILD 2: I'm going on a picnic and I'm taking an ant and a banana.

CHILD 1: I'm going on a picnic and I'm taking an ant, a banana, and a canoe.

Riddles. Riddles are age-old favorites for demonstrating the power of effective listening:

YOU: Three frogs were sitting on a log. One had a notion to jump off. How many were left?

CHILD: Two?

You: No, three. One just had a notion. He didn't jump.

There are many books with age-appropriate riddles that children will enjoy. Take a trip to the children's section of the library or the local book store to find some good choices.

Listening Skills

Think of listening as a skill, just like throwing a ball or riding a bicycle: We can learn how to do it, we become stronger with practice, and some people develop the skill to a stronger degree than others.

At the most primitive listening level, children must learn to tell the difference between sounds. They must learn the difference between the sound of their parents' voices and dogs barking outside or the radio playing music in another room. They learn to discriminate the tones others use in talking with them—when it's important to drop everything and listen, and when that isn't necessary.

Anyone who has spent time with a child with an attention deficit hyperactivity disorder (ADHD) can see in a very dramatic way how the inability to discriminate which sounds are important and which aren't can be a problem. For example, a first-grade teacher shows one of her students a picture of a cow with five legs and asks: "What is wrong with this picture?"

Johnny answers, "Bad muffler."

The teacher, thinking that she had perhaps not understood what Johnny had said or that Johnny had misunderstood the question, repeats the question.

Johnny repeats: "Bad muffler. That car outside the building has a bad muffler."

Perhaps the teacher wasn't even aware that there was a car outside the school making bad muffler sounds, because she had learned long ago to tune out irrelevant sounds. But to Johnny, the sound the car was making competed equally with the sounds coming from the teacher's mouth.

Even after children have learned to discriminate sounds, they must learn to understand the information *in* those sounds. Children learn the difference between a cat's affectionate purr and an angry hiss very early in life, because pain is a very effective teacher. Even preverbal toddlers learn the difference between affectionate and angry tones.

Later, children begin to interpret the words others use in conjunction with the tones to form a more complete understanding. For example, in a popular children's movie, the villainess says to the child: "Come here, my precious," and even very young children understand from her tone of voice that the woman intends to hurt the child. By the time children are in first grade, most have developed very sophisticated abilities to discriminate word and tone and to understand the intent of what is said as well as the actual words.

Sustained Listening

We know that many factors affect a child's ability to listen for long periods of time, such as:

- the intensity of environmental noise,
- the rhythm of environmental noise,
- the number of competing sounds,
- the temperature of the room, and
- the quality of the light.

But there are also factors within children that affect their ability to listen:

- general health,
- emotional state, and
- level of interest.

Active Listening

Active listening involves not only trying to understand what others say, but taking steps to extract as much information as possible. Active listening is, for the most part, a skill children in first grade are trying to develop. By the time children are in middle school and certainly by high school, their active listening skills should have evolved to the point that they can:

- Show their teachers they're listening.
- Reflect back what they have heard.
- Ask pertinent questions to clarify misunderstandings or to obtain more information.
- Communicate the value of the information.

Although very few first graders are able to display such sophisticated active listening skills, most should be able to begin building toward such skills by looking at the speaker and asking pertinent questions.

What Tests May Ask

Standardized tests at the first-grade level assess the ability to listen in a very straightforward manner, typically emphasizing accurate recounting of facts the students have heard.

During a standardized test, the teacher will read a statement or story to the children, who must then answer questions that determine how well they listened. Some questions simply require children to recount facts; others require both an understanding of the facts and the ability to draw inferences from what they have heard.

Practice Skill: Listening Skills

Directions: Say the following: "Listen to the following paragraph and then choose the correct answer to the following questions."

Read the following: Rosanne was going to see her grandparents. She had never been in an airplane before, and the man with the seat next to the window switched seats with her so that she could look out and see the white mountain tops.

1 Where was Rosanne going?
- Ⓐ to see her grandparents
- Ⓑ to the mountains
- Ⓒ to the beach
- Ⓓ back home to her parents

2 What did she see when she looked out the window?
- Ⓐ the ocean
- Ⓑ her grandparents' house
- Ⓒ her house
- Ⓓ the mountain tops

3 Why were the mountain tops the color they were?
- Ⓐ There were trees on the mountains.
- Ⓑ The sun was very bright.
- Ⓒ Rosanne was flying at night.
- Ⓓ There was snow on the mountain tops.

(See page 111 for answer key.)

Language Skills

Remember that in Chapter 3 we made a distinction between receptive vocabulary (the words we understand when we hear them) and expressive vocabulary (the words we actually use). These two types of vocabulary skills are actually components of larger skill areas referred to as *receptive language* (the language we understand) and *expressive language* (the language we use). Listening requires receptive language.

One of the most important early language skills for learning is the ability to distinguish which sounds are and aren't important. By the time they enter first grade, most children are able to discriminate what spoken information is important and what isn't.

For example:

Three girls went to the movies and paid $1 each for their tickets. Each girl had brought $5. How much in all did they spend on tickets?

The pertinent information in this passage is that there were three girls and each spent $1 on movie tickets. The fact that each girl brought $5 is unimportant in answering the question, and an effective listener will make that distinction.

For children to be able to discriminate important from unimportant information, they must:

- Understand the information they've been given.
- Understand the structure of the questions.
- Understand the way they should express their answers.

What Tests May Ask

As part of the effort to assess listening skills, most standardized tests ask children to understand the information they've been given and answer questions based on that information in the proper form.

Practice Skill: Language Skills

Directions: Choose the correct answers to the following questions.

4 Millie wants to build a bird house. What does she need to do that?
- Ⓐ a bird
- Ⓑ a hammer
- Ⓒ a camera
- Ⓓ a bird house

5 Sally took her dog Sue to the animal hospital. Who is Sue?
- Ⓐ a little girl
- Ⓑ a dog
- Ⓒ a squirrel
- Ⓓ an animal doctor

6 The teacher gave a piece of white paper to Tom, who was wearing a blue shirt. What did the teacher give to Tom?
- Ⓐ a piece of blue paper
- Ⓑ a blue shirt
- Ⓒ a piece of white paper
- Ⓓ a headache

7 Billy and his brother Tom camped out in their backyard. They only had one tent. Which picture shows what happened?

Ⓐ Ⓑ Ⓒ Ⓓ

(See page 111 for answer key.)

CHAPTER 6

Language Mechanics

Language mechanics refers to those seemingly little things that make the written word easier to understand. In first grade, that includes the basics of capitalization, punctuation, and word usage.

What Your First Grader Should Be Learning

By the time most children enter first grade, they have mastered most of the basics of standard communication. They know, for example, that their statements should contain subjects, actions, and objects, although they aren't familiar with terms such as *noun*, *verb*, and so on. They may know that lowercase letters exist, but most don't know anything about the rules for when to use uppercase and when to use lowercase letters.

Most children enter first grade able to speak and understand simple, standard language, but their ability to use correct language in writing is nearly nonexistent at first. Even by the end of first grade, their ability to express themselves in writing is limited to very simple, basic skills. As a result, expectations for their performance on standardized tests are limited.

How You Can Help Your Child

Children model and understand the language they hear. That might not seem to be a terribly radical concept to most parents, yet many persist in speaking a sort of "baby talk" to children even into their teens.

Don't Use Baby Talk. There is a growing body of evidence that speaking in a type of baby talk to preverbal and early-verbal children may indeed help them acquire language skills. But by the time children are in kindergarten and first grade, the usefulness of such language has long since passed. It's not necessary to speak in Elizabethan English to children or to speak in highly artificial, professorial tones. But do try to avoid the strained affectations you used when they were younger. For example, instead of saying:

"Jackie, Mommy wants 'oo to go with her to eat pusgetti."

you should say:

"Jackie, let's go out and eat spaghetti."

While you're at it, discourage other well-meaning adults from speaking in "baby-ese."

Explain Dialect. When you read stories with regional dialog to your first grader, point out that the language is not technically correct, but that's how people in some parts of the country or in other countries speak.

For example, if you are reading from a Joel Chandler Harris story, you might point out that the dialog is in the dialect of the deep South from more than 100 years ago. If you're reading a story that takes place in Ireland, point out that the dialect is Irish.

Read! In any case, you can't read too much to your children. Read a variety of materials. Hearing the natural rhythms and sentence structures of standard language will help children become accustomed to them, and they will model them in their own speaking and writing.

Don't Obsess. Don't worry too much about capitalization and punctuation in first grade. You may wish to point out simple rules, such as the practice of capitalizing the first letter of the first word in a sentence and the first letter of proper nouns; the addition of a period at the end of a declarative sentence, a question mark at the end of a sentence that asks a question, and an exclamation mark at the end of a sentence making a strong statement.

Write! Encourage your first graders to write. They can write thank you-notes to their grandparents for presents, they can add their own P.S. to letters you're writing to relatives, or they can find pen pals.

Buy your first grader a diary, or buy or download a computer-based diary program, such as Parson Technology's Daily Journal program. Again, their entries won't be terribly sophisticated, and they may need help in writing down their own thoughts and reading what they have written. But writing down their thoughts will get them into the habit of doing so.

Many children also enjoy making up their own stories, but may not have the writing skills to write them on paper or on a computer word processor. Let them dictate stories to you while you write them or type them into a word processor, or sit with them while they write and help them with words they don't know how to spell. Point out when they omit capitals and punctuation, and help them proofread what they have written.

Spellcheck Alert

One note of caution about word processors is in order. The more sophisticated word processing software programs have auto-correct features that frequently spot common spelling, capital-

ization, and punctuation errors and automatically correct them for you. Turn off this feature when your child uses the computer. It's fine to leave mistake alerts turned on; that may even help your child learn to recognize mistakes.

For example, several of the more sophisticated word processors will highlight words that aren't in their dictionaries, either by turning them a special color (usually red) or by making some other mark, such as underlining them in red. Be very careful with computer word processors designed for adults. Their many features are frequently very confusing to adults, and they may absolutely overwhelm children.

What Tests May Ask

This chapter outlines language mechanics skills that your child may be presented with on standardized tests. In addition, we describe how standardized tests assess these skills, as this format is typically different from how they are assessed within the classroom.

Capitalization

Many early first graders know that there are such things as lowercase letters, but most are still printing in capital letters until their teachers begin to insist that they learn lowercase.

What Your First Grader Is Learning

By the end of first grade, your child should be able to recognize and print all uppercase and lowercase letters in simple, block format. She should understand that the first word in a sentence begins with a capital letter, as does the first letter of a proper noun.

First graders are unlikely to understand more complex capitalization rules, such as capitalizing the first letter of the first word in an independent clause following a colon. Testing knowledge of capitalization involves presenting sentences and asking children to pick which words should be capitalized.

Practice Skill: Capitalization

Directions: Read the following sentences. Then pick the words that should be capitalized.

---

1 Willie gave mary the new ball.

- Ⓐ gave
- Ⓑ ball
- Ⓒ mary
- Ⓓ new

---

2 katie dropped her pencil onto the floor.

- Ⓐ katie
- Ⓑ pencil
- Ⓒ onto
- Ⓓ floor

---

3 Sally went to france in an airplane for a holiday.

- Ⓐ holiday
- Ⓑ france
- Ⓒ went
- Ⓓ airplane

(See page 111 for answer key.)

Punctuation

Early first graders won't punctuate their sentences, and even they will have problems reading their own writing as a result. Typically, they won't notice punctuation, but will read as if all the sentences are run-ons.

What Your First Grader Is Learning

By the end of first grade, most children will have progressed only to periods, question marks, exclamation marks, and apostrophes showing possession. When it comes to apostrophes, they will typically only understand those of the *'s* variety (such as "Johnny's"). They won't understand single-ending apostrophes used with nouns ending in *s*, *x*, *ce*, or *z* sounds (such as Willis' or Oz').

Forget trying to teach first graders more sophisticated punctuation such as commas, and don't even think of expecting them to understand colons, semicolons, and dashes. At this age, most are able to understand the concept of beginnings and endings of sentences, but most are unable to understand independent and dependent clauses, parenthetical material, and so on.

What Tests May Ask

Typical standardized test questions aimed at punctuation on the first-grade level focus on very simple examples. They present a series of sentences and ask which one is punctuated correctly.

Practice Skill: Punctuation

Directions: Read each question and choose the correct answer.

---

4 Which sentence has the period in the right place?

- Ⓐ Johnny took. his dog to class
- Ⓑ Johnny took his dog to class.
- Ⓒ Johnny took his dog. to class
- Ⓓ Johnny. took his dog to class

---

5 Choose the sentence with the correct punctuation.

Ⓐ Where did Donna go today

Ⓑ Where did Donna go today.

Ⓒ Where did Donna go today?

Ⓓ Where did Donna go today!

6 Choose the sentence with the correct punctuation.

Ⓐ The house is on fire?

Ⓑ The house is on fire,

Ⓒ The house is on fire!

Ⓓ The house is on fire

(See page 111 for answer key.)

Usage

Many children experience problems identifying the correct forms of words even by the end of first grade. For example, many Americans incorrectly say "between you and *I*," rather than the technically correct "between you and *me*." When someone asks, "Who is it?" even most adults respond with the technically incorrect, "It's *me*," rather than the correct but awkward sounding version, "It is *I*."

What Your First Grader Is Learning

By the end of first grade, your child should be able to use correct tense (such as *say* vs. *said*), numeration (such as "one *man* and two *men*"), and superlatives (such as *big*, *bigger*, and *biggest*) of common, simple words.

What Tests May Ask

Standardized tests assess how well your child understands usage by presenting simple sentences and asking children to fill in a blank with the correct form of the verb, superlative, or number.

Practice Skill: Usage

Directions: Fill in the blank in each sentence.

7 Lisa ___ in first grade.

Ⓐ be

Ⓑ are

Ⓒ is

Ⓓ were

8 James is _____ than his brother.

Ⓐ taller

Ⓑ tallest

Ⓒ tall

Ⓓ talled

9 Yesterday I saw one man. Today I saw two ___.

Ⓐ man

Ⓑ men

Ⓒ mans

Ⓓ mens

(See page 111 for answer key.)

Pronouns

First graders may have a very difficult time understanding the concept of pronouns. They may understand that we refer to boys as *he* and to girls as *she*, but when asked to demonstrate this concept in written exercises, they may not always make correct choices.

Children who still use immature speech ("Me don't want to go") or whose parents engage in immature speech patterns when talking with them will need strong modeling and reinforcement for correct pronoun use before they can make proper pronoun choices.

Practice Skill: Pronouns

Directions: Read these sentences and choose the correct pronouns for the underlined words.

---

10 <u>Earl and Marie</u> live in a big house.

   Ⓐ Them   Ⓑ They

   Ⓒ Us   Ⓓ We

---

11 I rode <u>my bicycle</u> to school.

   Ⓐ her   Ⓑ it

   Ⓒ him   Ⓓ my

---

12 Mother gave <u>Shawna and me</u> ice cream.

   Ⓐ we   Ⓑ them

   Ⓒ they   Ⓓ us

(See page 111 for answer key.)

Sentences

Most young children think in a very simple, concrete manner. By early first grade, they think and speak in simple sentences; by late first grade most are able to write simple sentences with a noun and a verb, such as, "The dog ran" or "The sky is blue." They may well be confused by:

- compound and complex sentences

- parenthetical material, such as "Mary, <u>my friend from school</u>, has a new dog."

- unusual arrangement of elements, such as "Up went the balloon."

Practice Skill: Sentences

Directions: Read each of these sentences and then choose the correct sentence that goes with it.

---

13 The puppy drank the water.

   Ⓐ Did puppy the water drink?

   Ⓑ Did the puppy drink the water?

   Ⓒ Did water the puppy drink?

   Ⓓ Did the water drink the puppy?

---

14 Did you see the airplane?

   Ⓐ Yes, I seed the airplane.

   Ⓑ Yes, I see the airplane.

   Ⓒ Yes, I sawed the airplane.

   Ⓓ Yes, I saw the airplane.

---

15 Is Sam Mary's brother?

   Ⓐ Yes, him is her brother.

   Ⓑ Yes, he is her brother.

   Ⓒ Yes, he is she brother.

   Ⓓ Yes, him is she brother.

(See page 111 for answer key.)

Paragaphs

Understanding paragraphs requires sophisticated, logical thinking skills that many first graders still don't possess. Indeed, many children this age are still struggling to understand where sentences begin and end.

What Your Child Is Learning

Many first-grade curricula do not place much emphasis on distinguishing the cut-offs among paragraphs. Instead, most first-grade teachers are content to work on having their students write simple, correct sentences. At first-grade level, most children are able to understand some of the basic concepts that they will build on in later grades when they are able to more fully understand paragraphs, mainly the concept of sentences that tell about the same thing.

What Tests May Ask

Standardized tests assess a child's ability to understand paragraphs by giving them a few sample sentences, and asking them to choose another sentence that goes along with the same thought.

Practice Skill: Paragraphs

Directions: Look at the sentences. They tell about the same thing. Then look at the choices and choose the sentence that also tells about the same thing.

16 My sister and I wanted to ride our bikes. But it was raining.

   Ⓐ My birthday will be on Saturday this year.

   Ⓑ I am older than my sister.

   Ⓒ I have a new little brother.

   Ⓓ So we put together a puzzle.

17 My dog's name is Baxter. He is brown and white. He is a basset.

   Ⓐ It snowed today.

   Ⓑ I am in first grade.

   Ⓒ I am six years old.

   Ⓓ We like to go for walks.

(See page 111 for answer key.)

CHAPTER 7

Spelling

Oh, for a language with regular, consistent spelling rules! We can't help but envy children in Spanish-speaking countries, who, after learning a small number of rules, can spell any word in the language when they hear it. Because English is a blended language, with so many important words from so many different languages, even educated adults must frequently run to the dictionary or rely heavily on their computerized spell-check features.

Although many school districts avoid teaching spelling in first grade because of misguided fears that it will somehow dampen writing creativity, we know for a fact that it's far easier to teach correct spelling right off than try to fix ingrained faulty spelling later.

What Your First Grader Should Be Learning

It's not unusual at all for early first graders to be clueless when it comes to spelling. Even late first graders (and second, third, and fourth graders) continue to experience many problems in spelling, especially if they were not taught spelling in the early grades.

With luck, early first graders have mastered writing the alphabet and are secure in the knowledge that A comes before F, V comes after J, and so on.

By late first grade, children are ready to spell simple, whole words. Basic one- and two-syllable words, such as "dog," "car," and "father," are typical of the words late first graders will be able to spell.

Vowels and consonants are a bit more complex. In early first grade, children have little concept of the use of vowels as anything other than placeholders. But by middle to late first grade, they will begin to understand that vowels combine with consonants to make sounds.

How You Can Help Your Child

The most important way to help your first grader develop spelling is to recognize that any curriculum that totally ignores the teaching of standard spelling in first grade is misguided. It's much more difficult to change ingrained incorrect spelling than to teach correct spelling from the beginning. Think of teaching spelling as one area of education that is just common sense.

True, you can turn children against learning proper spelling if you approach it in a boring manner. But it's possible to simultaneously allow children to learn to write without undue emphasis on perfection while teaching proper spelling.

If your child isn't receiving spelling instruction in first grade, the burden may fall on you. Remember to keep it fun. Spelling doesn't have to be drudgery, punitive, or humiliating. The more innovative things you can think of to do with spelling, the better.

Home-School Spelling

Find a book or series of materials for parents who home-school their children, and consider teaching spelling to be something you do in a sort of home-schooling arrangement. Find some exercises in spelling that you and your first grader can practice for a few minutes each day. Remember, you don't have to be Dickensian about it. You're still dealing with a young child who needs to run and play, not stay indoors all day learning how to spell.

Texture Words

Take an old cake pan or dish pan and partially fill it with fine, clean sand. Give your child a word and have him "write" the word in the sand.

Food Words

Give your children some cookie cutters in the form of letters and let them cut out letters in bread, soft cheese, pancakes, or Jell-O. Have them put the letters together to form words.

Scrabble Junior

The children's version of the *Scrabble* game (*Scrabble Junior*) actually prints each letter of the word on the board, together with a picture of the word in the first square. Children simply match up letters in their hand to the letters on the board—a fun way to learn to spell!

Flash Cards

Ask your teacher if there is a state spelling list for first grade, or consult lists of high-frequency words for ideas. These are frequently written to match the vocabulary on standardized tests, so first-grade lists will provide a strong match for the types of words most first graders in your state should know (and that later teachers will expect). If your school resists teaching spelling, you may have to insist on having a copy of the list, or you may have to find someone with a first grader at another school who can obtain it. Alternatively, take a look at a children's book for common words. Many early readers also provide lists of common words. Using any of these resources, you can make your own flash cards.

Make two piles, one of words your child has spelled correctly and another stack of those spelled incorrectly. When you have gone through

the original stack, shuffle the words in each of the new stacks and go through them again.

Continue the flash cards from the missed words pile and have your child repeat the correct spelling before moving on to the next card. Repeating the correct spelling is an important way to turn it into a habit. After your child has spelled a word correctly a certain number of times in a row, put the card away (but occasionally return to those words).

Decorate!

Remember that the best way to remember something is to make it memorable. Give your child a spelling word. Have her print it in the center of the page, and then decorate it—add curlicues, color it, make a fancy design or draw a picture. Repeat for every word.

Label, Label

Take a cue from veteran kindergarten teachers and put labels on items around your house. For example, use the backs of old business cards or cut note cards and put the label "television" on the TV and "desk" on the desk. Your child will become accustomed to seeing the words spelled correctly and will more quickly learn to spell them.

Make Up Sentences

Writing complex original stories using spelling words may tax the talents of most first graders, but most can manage to write a sentence using a spelling word. Say the word, and have the child write the word in a sentence. The funnier or sillier the sentence, the better! Then see if the child can include four or five spelling words in one sentence. The key here is playfulness; make this seem like a game, not drudgery.

What to Expect with Today's Tests

Unfortunately, expressive spelling is very difficult to assess using the multiple-choice format common in tests using machine-scored answer sheets. As computer-administered tests become more widespread, children will be able to hear the word and see a picture of the thing to be spelled and then type in the spelling.

Standardized tests at this stage typically assess knowledge of expressive spelling by giving a list of incorrectly spelled words together with one correctly spelled word, and asking the child to choose the correct spelling.

Spelling Skills

Children may remember having seen a poster with an A next to a picture of an apple in their kindergarten class, but noting that the *A* can make different sounds (as in *skate*, *hall*, and *hat*) isn't emphasized in kindergarten because many children aren't developmentally ready to learn such skills at that age.

By the time they are ready to start first grade, most youngsters are ready to begin to spell simple words. At first, they are ready to learn familiar spellings, such as their names, a pet's name, and common nouns such as "mother" and "dad."

Vowels

By late first grade, your child should begin to understand that vowels combine with consonants to make sounds. For example, he will learn that the "g-o" in the middle of a word can make the sound as in "gopher" or as in "got," while "g-a" within words can make the sound as in "gate" or as in "gas."

Consonants

Next, most first graders begin to master consonants. For example, they learn that the *k* sound is made either by the *k* or, sometimes, the *c* (although they will probably not be ready to learn more esoteric sources such as *que* as in *unique*).

What You and Your Child Can Do

To help your child understand vowels, write the alphabet on a large piece of paper. Have your child circle all the vowels. Or retrieve an old, easy reader from the basement and have your child circle all the vowels in the story.

What Tests May Ask

Standardized tests in first grade assess spelling by giving a word (often as part of a sentence) and having a child fill in the missing letter, or by having the child choose the correctly spelled word from among a group of incorrectly spelled items. Tests may also provide a picture and then ask the child to choose the first letter of that word.

Practice Skill: Spelling Skills

Directions: Choose the letters that fill in the blanks in the following sentences.

1 This is a _oat. What goes in the blank?

Ⓐ g

Ⓑ t

Ⓒ k

Ⓓ t

2 Here are Mary and Katie. Mary is big. Katie is li__le. What letters go in the blank?

Ⓐ gg

Ⓑ dd

Ⓒ ll

Ⓓ tt

3 The _ _ ck swam in the water.

Ⓐ do

Ⓑ tu

Ⓒ du

Ⓓ go

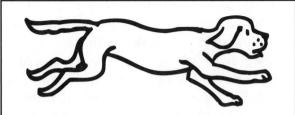

4 The _ _ g ran down the street.

Ⓐ du   Ⓑ to

Ⓒ do   Ⓓ tu

Directions: Choose the correct answer for the following questions.

5 Choose the word that is spelled correctly:

Ⓐ buk   Ⓑ boke

Ⓒ book   Ⓓ bkoo

6 Choose the correct spelling:

Ⓐ kat   Ⓑ qat

Ⓒ cta   Ⓓ cat

7 Choose the vowel that starts the name of the picture.

Ⓐ e   Ⓑ o

Ⓒ a   Ⓓ l

8 Choose the consonant that starts the name of the picture.

Ⓐ w   Ⓑ l

Ⓒ h   Ⓓ e

(See page 111 for answer key.)

CHAPTER 8

Math Concepts

You can't teach your child mathematical concepts in one day. Learning this skill is an ongoing process that requires a steady emphasis over a long period of time. Still, there are some things you can do right away to help prepare your child for standardized tests.

One of the most important things you can do is to show that math can be fun. That may sound glib, but you'd be surprised how many Americans have decided that math is just too hard and that it's perfectly normal to hate the subject. This problem is particularly widespread among girls.

Unfortunately, many girls today believe they are just "naturally" terrible at math. If you can make math fun, you'll have taken a huge first step toward improving your child's ultimate test scores.

How You Can Help Your Child

How do you make math fun? It's not hard with kids this age. First graders are still Great Pretenders. They enjoy playing store, pretending to be characters from *Star Wars*, or holding Beanie Baby pet shows. You can use this love of play very effectively in teaching a variety of number concepts.

One of the best ways to do this is with money. Some parents have had great success actual coins and paper money, while others use Monopoly money to play "store" with their child. You can teach a wide range of basic math skills this way. Here's what you can do with this sort of learning play with a "hot dog store."

PARENT: Hi, do you sell hot dogs?

CHILD: I sure do.

PARENT: My son is having some friends come for a barbecue for the Fourth of July. We will need enough for six children.

CHILD: Your little boy will probably like these hot dogs. They're delicious.

PARENT: Great. How much are they?

CHILD: They are usually 5 cents apiece. But if you buy 20, I'll give you a special price. Say 20 for one dollar?

PARENT: Hey, wait a minute. That's the same price!

CHILD [puzzled]: It is?

This scenario demonstrates several principles you'll need to understand in dealing with youngsters this age.

- They imitate what they see: The child does a good job of imitating how a store clerk would offer special deals.

- The son grossly underpriced the hot dogs. Don't become too disturbed if your first grader is pretending to sell a new Chevy van off the pretend showroom floor for $10. At this age, accuracy of the pricing is not as important as knowing that if Susie sells both husband and wife $10 Chevy vans, she needs to get $20 from them.

- Most first graders won't realize that offering 20 hot dogs for $1 is the same as selling them for a nickel apiece. Your first grader's lack of familiarity with this relatively sophisticated operation gives you the opportunity to teach.

You might want to use this example as a chance to demonstrate to your child that you can get the same monetary value using different combinations of coins. Here's how:

PARENT: Do you remember how many pennies are the same as a nickel?

CHILD: Yeah. It takes five pennies to equal a nickel.

PARENT: OK. We are going to see if charging a nickel apiece for the hot dogs is the same as charging one dollar for 20. Let's see. Here are 20 nickels. [Put 20 nickels on the counter.]

CHILD: That's how much it costs for 20 hot dogs without my special deal.

PARENT: Right. Now let's try something. I'm going to replace all of these nickels with pennies. Let's start with this first nickel. If I take away the nickel, how many pennies do I have to put in its place?

CHILD: Put five in its place.

PARENT: Right. Now let's pick up this next nickel. How many pennies do I have to put in its place?

CHILD: Five.

PARENT: Right. Now I want you to help me. Let's take up these nickels one at a time and put five pennies in each nickel's place.

CHILD: All right!

[Continue until you and your child have replaced all nickels with pennies.]

PARENT: Good job. How many pennies do you think we put in place of the nickels?

CHILD: I don't know.

PARENT: Let's see. [Parent and child count the pennies.] Wow! There were 100 pennies. Now, let's see. That means that, if you bought 20 hot dogs at the regular price of one nickel each,

that would be 20 nickels, which is the same as how many pennies?

CHILD: That's the same as 100 pennies.

PARENT: Right. And 100 pennies is the same as . . . what?

CHILD: 20 nickels is the same as one dollar.

PARENT: Right!

If you charged a nickel in the pennies and nickels game, your child may still not be able to figure out that 5 times 20 equals 100 when you apply this to other things (such as 5 buckets with 20 apples in each). Still, you're preparing your child for logical problem solving, for which he will be ready shortly. Your first grader still enjoys playing with Mom and Dad and still thinks you are the most intelligent people in the world. You can apply the same spirit of play in other ways.

Pet Shows

Let's say the kids in your child's neighborhood like to hold mock pet shows. Although these contests always end with the winner being the one the other girls liked the most, this scenario could present an opportunity to teach; help them narrow the contest down to five finalists and then have a reading of "fifth place," then "fourth place," and so on.

At the Store

Bring your daughter with you to the wholesale club when you are buying cases of bottled water. You note that you can buy 16 one-liter bottles for $6.99 or 32 half-liter bottles for $8.99. Pull out your calculator and show your child how to calculate how much each liter costs in each case. You can then make a game of seeing how much you can "beat the store" by making the most economical purchases, and even keep a record of how much you saved on this trip.

If your attempts to apply logic in reasoning with a first grader seem to fall on deaf ears, don't despair: Your child is probably not quite ready in first grade to understand logical principles. Typically, she will begin to understand logic sometime in first or second grade.

What to Expect with Today's Tests

The standardized tests your first grader is likely to face are designed to assess a number of skills, including:

- numeration,
- sequencing,
- number concepts,
- patterns and place value, and
- problem solving.

In addition, math tests include some information that isn't necessary to find the correct answer, to make sure that students are able to discriminate relevant from irrelevant detail. For example, a test may ask: "Jeffrey has $2, Darla has $3, and Terry has $1. Jeffrey is 5 years old, Darla is 8 years old, and Terry is 2 years old. How much money do they have in all?" Obviously, their ages have nothing to do with the money they have. You can play little informal games with your child, teaching him to be on guard for such tricks. For example, consider the following riddle:

You: You're driving a bus. Three people get on at First Street. Seven people get on at Fifth Street. Two people get on at Eleventh Avenue. How old is the bus driver?

Child: I don't know; 25?

You: No, 6; I said that *you* were driving a bus.

TIP

Test questions are now making increasing use of graphs, number lines, and charts. Make sure that your child knows how to read them.

Numeration

Standardized math tests assess numeration, or how well your child understands basic numbers. For first graders, the tests generally include easy items (such as counting five puppies) up to more difficult questions (such as counting beyond 100).

What Your First Grader Is Learning

Early first graders should be able to count to 10, and by the end of first grade they should be able to count to 100. In addition, an early first grader can handle fairly sophisticated symbolic functions; in other words, she realizes for the first time, for example, that the number "6" stands for a quantity of six.

Remember, however, that first graders base their beliefs on what they *sense* to be true, rather than on what logic or rational thought would tell them. This is why a beginning first grader may think that a nickel is worth more than a dime because it's bigger.

What You and Your Child Can Do

Practice, practice, practice. The more your child is exposed to even the most basic number concepts, the better. Use everyday objects around the house to practice counting. Write down a number and then ask your child to select that number of grapes, cherries, or M&Ms. If your child is right, she gets to eat the answer!

When you go to the store, send your child out on "food expeditions." You can say: "Go get me three oranges...four lemons...and two cans of cat food." Or write down the number, and then have her fetch the amount of groceries you indicate. If you're really industrious, make up a list before you leave home, and draw the item together with the number that you want the child to select.

Practice Skill: Numeration

Directions: Look at the following pictures and answer the questions.

1 How many puppies are there?

  Ⓐ 2   Ⓑ 4

  Ⓒ 6   Ⓓ 8

2 How many trees are there?

  Ⓐ 2   Ⓑ 4

  Ⓒ 5   Ⓓ 11

3 How many cats are in the box?

  Ⓐ 3   Ⓑ 6

  Ⓒ 5   Ⓓ 8

4 Which dog is the biggest?

  Ⓐ first picture

  Ⓑ middle picture

  Ⓒ last picture

(See pages 111–112 for answer key.)

Sequencing

Sequencing involves placing things first, second, third, fourth, and so on. It also means knowing what numbers are bigger than or smaller than other numbers.

What Your First Grader Is Learning

Early first graders may have no concept of sequencing beyond "first" and "last," but by the end of first grade, they should know ordinal positions up to 100. In other words, they should not only know that 2 is bigger than 1, but that 99 is bigger than 96, and that 96 is smaller than 97. In addition, they should know "between" (as in, "The cow is between the tree and the fence.").

What You and Your Child Can Do

Sequencing can be fun to play. If your child has a collection (we'll use Beanie Babies here, but anything will do—shells, stamps, and so on), work on sequencing. Start out with just two objects.

1. Line up Pinky the Flamingo and Fetch the Golden Retriever.

2. Ask your child: "Which Beanie Baby is first, and which is second?"

3. Now add the Princess bear. Make up a contest and award first, second, and third places. Keep adding Beanie Babies and see if your child knows which is which.

Awards

If you and your child are really creative and have extra time, you could have your child design first, second, and third place "ribbons" and award them to various stuffed animals for a variety of contests. Try athletic contests, size contests, and so on.

Vet Clinic

If your child has small plastic toy animals, set up a pretend vet clinic. Line up the small animals. Have the nurse announce each animal's turn to see the vet by saying, "Next." Ask your child which animal is "next" in line.

What Tests May Ask

Standardized tests at this level typically assess whether your child has any concept of order (what comes first, second, and last), up to fairly complex sequencing activities.

Practice Skill: Sequencing

Directions: Choose the correct answers for the following problems.

5 Which one is between the girl and the cow?

ⓐ cat   ⓑ pig

ⓒ dog   ⓓ boy

---

6 The cat, pig, girl, dog, cow, and boy stop at a house. The lady who lives there lets them in one at a time. After the girl goes in, the lady comes to the door and says, "Next." Which is next?

ⓐ cat   ⓑ pig

ⓒ dog   ⓓ cow

(See pages 111–112 for answer key.)

Number Concepts

Standardized tests at this age require that your child solve a range of word problems, from very easy to relatively sophisticated. In addition, tests at this level typically expect a primitive understanding of basic measurements such as feet, inches, time, and monetary units; and such quantifiers as "dozen."

What Your First Grader Is Learning

Early first graders are still functioning at a fairly concrete level of understanding when it comes to number concepts. Usually, you can fool them when figuring out quantity problems on the basis of "how big" rather than "how many." For example, if there are 5 large adult dogs in one group and 7 small puppies in another group, early first graders may say there are more adult dogs than puppies.

Your child will probably begin first grade without knowing much about different measurement units (such as English versus metric measures of length, volume, and weight). For example, in counting inches, your child may not yet understand that 12, not 10 or 100, equals one foot. By the end of first grade, your child should be able to translate 12 and 24 inches into 1 and 2 feet, but may still have trouble with fractions, such as 2 feet 3 inches.

What You and Your Child Can Do

While playing "store," you can have fun with number concepts. Select a number of items from the store. Now ask your child (the storekeeper) to add two more items to your pile on the counter. Ask your child to total the number of items you now have. Still in your pretend store, point to a pile of 6 lemons and a pile of 4 grapefruits. Ask your child which pile has more fruit. If she says "grapefruits," have her count each one out loud. Then have her count the lemons out loud. Explain the difference.

Practice Skill: Number Concepts

Directions: Choose the correct answers for the following questions.

7 Susie picked 12 apples and put them in her basket. Her father picked 7 more and put them in Susie's basket. How many apples does Susie have in her basket?

Ⓐ 11   Ⓑ 22

Ⓒ 19   Ⓓ 127

8 Are there more girls, more boys, or the same number of girls and boys?

Ⓐ the same number of girls and boys

Ⓑ more girls

Ⓒ more boys

9 Chris sold 12 boxes of doughnuts, Gina sold 5, Jean sold 18, and Royce sold 17. Who sold the most boxes of doughnuts?

Ⓐ Chris   Ⓑ Gina

Ⓒ Jean   Ⓓ Royce

10 Chris and Royce were trying to sell more than each other. How did this contest turn out?

Ⓐ Chris sold 5 more than Royce

Ⓑ Royce sold 12 more than Chris

Ⓒ Chris sold 12 more than Royce

Ⓓ Royce sold 5 more than Chris

11 Terry, Linda, and Maria collected cans for the food drive at their school. Terry collected 5 cans, Linda collected 12 cans, and Maria collected 11 cans. The food drive began on September 1 and ended on September 15. How many cans in all did Terry, Linda, and Maria collect?

Ⓐ 28   Ⓑ 14

Ⓒ 15   Ⓓ 100

12 Find the mystery number:
7 + ? = 10

(A) 7   (B) 3

(C) 8   (D) 17

13 Find the mystery number:
? − 3 = 7

(A) 4   (B) 7

(C) 10   (D) 13

(See pages 111–112 for answer key.)

Patterns and Place Value

Patterns (knowing which comes first, second, third, and so on) and place value (ones, tens, hundreds, thousands, and so on) are two fairly sophisticated concepts in mathematics.

What Your First Grader Is Learning

Many first graders begin school with no idea (or only a very primitive concept) of numbers, and they don't understand place value. By the end of first grade, they should have mastered elementary pattern concepts and have a tentative notion of place value.

What You and Your Child Can Do

Line up a variety of toys on a table. Ask your child to point to the "third object." Or, use small fruits (berries, cherries, and so on) and let the child eat the answer if she gets it right.

What Tests May Ask

Because first graders don't typically know much about place value, tests typically present a variety of patterns but place only minor emphasis on this skill.

Practice Skill: Patterns and Place Value

Directions: Choose the correct answers for the following questions.

14 Which apple does the arrow point to?

(A) 10th

(B) 12th

(C) 2nd

(D) 1st

15 The children in Ms. Allen's class had a race from the sliding board to the swings on the playground. Mary came in second place. Her friend Angela came in just a little ahead of Mary. What place did Angela finish?

(A) 3rd

(B) 1st

(C) 4th

(D) 5th

16 Jean is going to visit Jason, who lives in the 3rd house from the left. What is Jason's house number?

Ⓐ 101   Ⓑ 103   Ⓒ 105   Ⓓ 107

17 Fill in the blank: 2, 4, 6, ___, 10, 12

Ⓐ 5   Ⓑ 7

Ⓒ 8   Ⓓ 9

(See pages 111–112 for answer key.)

CHAPTER 9

Math Computation

You undoubtedly have noticed your preschooler's fascination with counting. She counts everything—the number of presents under the Christmas tree, the chairs around the dining room table, the number of freckles on Aunt Rosanne's nose. You probably became good friends with *Sesame Street's* Count and heard your children count "One—one puppy. Two—two puppies...ah, ah, ah."

What Your First Grader Should Be Learning

By the time children begin first grade, the fascination with counting has progressed to curiosity about addition and subtraction. Brittany may know that she had saved $12 for the toy she wants and if she can charm Grandmother into giving her $8 more, she can buy it. Tom knows that Grandpa gave him $5 for helping him rake the yard, and Grandma Jean gave him $5 for helping her feed the roses, so he now has $10.

First graders should be able to count to 100 by ones, twos, fives and tens, and should be able to write numerals to 100. Although there will be some notable exceptions, first graders' mathematics abilities are generally confined to addition and subtraction. (They should be able to add and subtract numbers up to and from 10.) Some late first graders are able to understand the notion of carrying, but many still do not understand this concept.

Remember that subtraction usually develops later than addition. Your first grader who knows that 5 + 3 = 8 may not understand that 8 − 3 = 5 until middle to late first grade.

Multiplication is beyond first grader's skills, and the concept of division is impossibly difficult for most.

How You Can Help Your Child

Our grandparents learned simple counting and subtraction using counting beads or buttons and number lines. Go into a veteran first-grade teacher's classroom, and you will see plastic containers with bright buttons and construction-paper number lines. These are still the best tools for teaching addition and subtraction.

Make an Abacus. The Chinese discovered very early in their history that addition and subtraction lend themselves very readily to counting frames with beads that slide along dowels or wires. Your first grader will not be able to understand the sophisticated abacus because it requires regrouping, but a simple dowel or wire with sliding beads will be easy enough for your child to understand.

You can make your own abacus very easily with something as simple as a shoestring and beads. If you want to teach Drew that 5 + 2 = 7, have him put five beads on the string and then add two more; then have him count them. If you want to teach Elizabeth that 9 − 3 = 6, have her first put nine beads on the string, then take away three; then have her count them.

Use Bean Counters. Teacher's supply houses and children's educational toy stores will sell brightly colored counting frames and slide counters. These also work well, but you don't have to spend money on these aids. You can accomplish the same teaching with objects such as beans, beads, buttons, coins, and so on.

Start with a bowl of beans. If you want to teach Cimmie that 4 + 3 = 7, have her start with a pile of four beans and a pile of three beans and then combine them and count them. If you want to teach Kellen that 7 – 5 = 2, then begin with a pile of seven buttons, take away five, and have her count the number remaining.

Play Computer Games. Computers may still be a mystery to you, but many kids are already software experts, even in first grade. There is a growing body of excellent computer software packages (such as *Math Blaster* and *Millie's Math House*) that can be helpful, especially if your child is fascinated by computers. Best of all, these packages present mathematical instruction in an engaging way that makes math fun for even the youngest child.

Model Math. Show your child that you use math every day. Let Rachel see your cash register receipt. Let Christie see you balance your checkbook. Show James how you count the change you receive at the fast-food restaurant. They won't be ready to perform these actions yet, but they will begin to see very early that math is important.

What to Expect with Today's Tests

Standardized tests of mathematical skills include items from the ridiculously easy to the impossibly difficult. Your first grader will probably see addition and subtraction items ranging from simple addition or subtraction of single digits with the answer less than 10, to addition and subtraction of two-digit numbers that require carrying. Most questions will be straightforward mathematical questions requiring your child to select the correct answer from a list of possibilities.

Adding Whole Numbers

Your first grader is rapidly developing addition skills. Generally, the sequence is this:

1. adding single digits with the sum less than or up to 10;
2. adding the single digits 1 to 9;
3. adding double digits without carrying.

Remember that your child won't learn skills in an orderly fashion; knowledge is usually gained on an erratic path. Try not to become frustrated if you see plateaus from time to time. There will probably be other periods in which your child will develop math skills very quickly.

What Tests May Ask

Standardized tests ask first graders questions about adding whole numbers, presenting the problems in several different ways. Problems may be presented this way:

$$\begin{array}{r} 3 \\ +3 \\ \hline \end{array}$$

Tests may also present problems this way:

$$3 + 3 = \underline{6}.$$

Practice Skill: Adding Whole Numbers

Directions: Look at these math problems and select the correct answers.

1. $\begin{array}{r} 5 \\ +3 \\ \hline \end{array}$

   Ⓐ 53   Ⓑ 35

   Ⓒ 8   Ⓓ 2

2   2
     +2

   Ⓐ 2   Ⓑ 4

   Ⓒ 5   Ⓓ 8

---

3   3 + 6 = ____

   Ⓐ 36   Ⓑ 9

   Ⓒ 3   Ⓓ 5

---

4   7 + 2 = __9__

   Ⓐ 9   Ⓑ 5

   Ⓒ 4   Ⓓ 8

(See page 112 for answer key.)

Subtracting Whole Numbers

Subtraction usually develops later than addition. First graders develop subtraction skills in the following sequence:

1. subtraction of a single digit from a larger single digit;

2. subtraction of a single digit from double digits, without regrouping;

3. subtraction of double digits from double digits, without regrouping.

Note that regrouping (also known as "borrowing") demands logical skills that are beyond the ability of many first graders. Don't panic if your first grader has no concept of borrowing! That will probably develop during second grade, when your child is ready for it. For now, concentrate on simple subtraction examples.

What Tests May Ask

Standardized tests include questions on subtracting whole numbers, and require your child to select the correct answer from a group of possibilities. Usually your child will be asked to subtract numbers in this format:

$$\begin{array}{r} 3 \\ -1 \\ \hline \end{array}$$

Other questions will present subtraction problems in this format:

$3 - 1 = \underline{2}$.

Practice Skill: Subtracting Whole Numbers

Directions: Read these math problems and select the correct answers.

5   6
     −2

   Ⓐ 8   Ⓑ 5

   Ⓒ 3   Ⓓ 4

---

6   15
     −3

   Ⓐ 12   Ⓑ 2

   Ⓒ 18   Ⓓ 8

---

7   29
     −17

Ⓐ 36

Ⓑ 2

Ⓒ 10

Ⓓ 12

8 8 − 2 = _____

Ⓐ 10   Ⓑ 6

Ⓒ 5   Ⓓ 7

(See page 112 for answer key.)

CHAPTER 10

Math Applications

Given the number of fascinating mathematics applications in everyday life, it's sometimes puzzling why so many people seem phobic about math. Even toymakers have found that fear of math is fashionable, and programmed a popular doll to say, "I hate math." Many of us have used math phobia as an excuse to avoid learning basic arithmetic. Adults who look down their noses at people who can't read will proudly boast that they don't know how to balance their checkbooks—and our children hear this. Is it any wonder so many youngsters say they hate math?

In this chapter, we explore some of the applications that not only show up on standardized tests but that children need to survive in the modern world.

What Your First Grader Should Be Learning

Math applications that first graders will begin to master include geometry, shapes, measurement, and word problems. By late kindergarten, children should be secure in their knowledge of basic, two-dimensional shapes such as triangles, squares, and rectangles.

By early first grade, students should be aware that there are more sophisticated shapes, such as pentagons, octagons, and so on. But they should also become aware that there are three-dimensional counterparts to the two-dimensional shapes: For example, circles in three-dimensional form become spheres, triangles become pyramids, and so on.

Most early first graders understand that there is a similarity between the shapes they see on paper (such as a sphere) and the shapes they encounter in real life (a beach ball).

How You Can Help Your Child

The most important strategy you can use in helping first graders strengthen their math application skills is to model a productive attitude toward math. If you are mathophobic, make a commitment to overcome your fear of math. There are many software packages available to drill you on math facts at the appropriate level, and there are excellent books for adults in the library on understanding math.

Let your child see for herself how you apply math in everyday life. For example, if you bowl or play golf, teach her how to fill out score cards. Show your child how you record the mileage on your car's odometer and the number of gallons you buy when you fill the tank with gas, and how you use that to see if your car's mileage changes. Involve your child in this and demonstrate how you figure out miles per gallon from one gas fill to the next. Or show your child how you make out a monthly budget and how you determine that you can spend a certain amount for eating out, horseback riding lessons, and so on.

Watch for examples in everyday life that show how you apply math. If you're watching a baseball game and the announcer gives a player's batting average or a pitcher's earned-run average, explain why these figures are important and demonstrate how to calculate them. When you watch the news and the report says that the Dow Jones Industrial Average went up or down and by how many points, explain why we follow the Dow and how we calculate the average.

Geometry

Geometry and the shapes that make up this part of math are all around us. It may seem shocking to you, but today's youngsters begin to learn about shapes—and to call it geometry—as early as kindergarten or first grade.

What Your First Grader Is Learning

Your child should be aware of the basic shapes of square, rectangle and circle; by early first grade, he should understand that there are more sophisticated shapes, such as pentagons, octagons, and so on. At the same time, he will learn that there are three-dimensional counterparts to the two-dimensional shapes, including spheres, pyramids, and cones.

What You and Your Child Can Do

Try using objects in your environment to review these shapes. For example, you could hold up a CD and a coin and point out that these two shapes are the same—both circles. Try finding shapes as you are driving down the highway. The house becomes a rectangle, the window a square. The streetlight may be a circle.

What Tests May Ask

Standardized tests ask straightforward questions about geometry and shapes that first graders should have mastered, such as asking children to identify which shapes are blocks, cones, and cubes.

Matching Shapes

Children at this age are often fascinated by shapes and will make a game of identifying shapes they see. As they drive to the beach, Miranda and Bryan will try to outdo each other at finding shapes: Bryan sees a propane gas tank in a backyard and announces that he sees a cylinder. Miranda counters that the road markers near the road construction they pass are cones.

What Tests May Ask

Standardized tests ask first graders to look at a basic shape, such as the drawing of a cube, and choose the picture that is most like the illustrated shape.

Practice Skills: Geometry and Shapes

Directions: Choose the correct answers for the following questions.

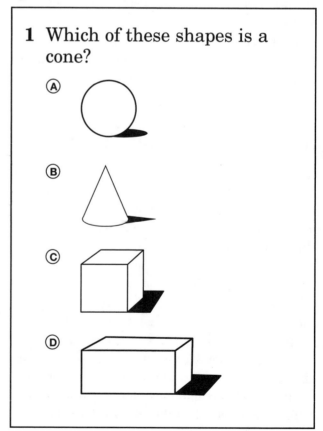

1 Which of these shapes is a cone?

Ⓐ

Ⓑ

Ⓒ

Ⓓ

2 Look at the shape below.

Choose the letter beside the picture that is most like the shape.

Ⓐ

Ⓑ

Ⓒ

Ⓓ

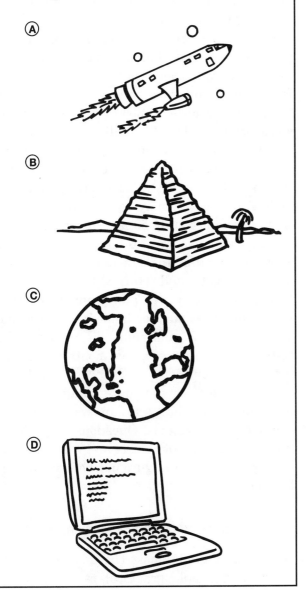

(See page 112 for answer key.)

Measurement

Before first grade, many children see measurement as an arbitrary practice—that using a tape measure before cutting a piece of cloth or measuring the amount of flour when making a cake is a random thing that an adult does. Hand your first grader a tape measure, however, and within an hour you will know that it is 18 feet from the kitchen stove to the clothes dryer, that the hamster is 6 inches long, and that it's 4 inches from baby brother's elbow to his wrist.

Early first graders will probably understand only round digits, such as 5 pounds, 18 inches, or 85 degrees. Don't worry about teaching fractions at this age; just be sure the child knows that we have means of making different measurements.

Most early first graders understand one-to-one correspondence, which will help them understand measurement. They will note that the person laying carpet measures carefully with a tape measure before cutting the carpet, and they will understand why the cashier at the grocery store weighs grapes before entering the price into the cash register.

Differentiating Among Measurement Instruments

Most children discover by late kindergarten to early first grade that there are different tools for measuring different things. For example, the tape measure that was appropriate for measuring the amount of chain Grandmother bought at the hardware store isn't appropriate for weighing the amount of cereal mix Dad bought at the market. The 16-ounce measuring cup that Uncle Bill used to measure out the amount of milk he needed for making rice pudding is not appropriate for measuring the number of pounds of potatoes his son John dug in the garden.

Standardized tests gauge your child's understanding of different measuring instruments by asking specific questions about various ways of measuring a variety of objects.

Reading a Calendar

We are becoming more and more dependent on calendars at a younger and younger age. The days when a first-grade teacher made a big show every morning of putting a star on the wall calendar to show us that it was January 29 or that we had 25 days of school left before the end of school have given way in many parts of the country to issuing each student a planner with pertinent school events and places for them to write down assignments.

Many early first graders still struggle with the names of the months, their orders, and the number of days. Few are able to independently flip through a new wall calendar and locate the month, much less the day of the month. But by late first grade, your child should be able to go to the calendar and find a date, or be able to identify it if someone points to one.

Coin Values

By middle first grade, most children have learned the values of coins up to one dollar. They should understand by that time that a dime is worth 10 cents, while a quarter is worth 25 cents. Early first graders will probably not be able to make change or understand combinations of coins, such as two dimes and a nickel equaling the same value as a quarter.

Standardized test questions of this type in first grade typically attempt to determine whether children can distinguish one coin from another and they can identify a one-dollar bill. They usually also check whether children can calculate the values of simple coin combinations.

Telling Time

With the advent of digital clocks, many children have learned to tell time on them before beginning first grade. But even many middle to late first graders are not firm in their ability to read time on analog clocks, even if they have large numbers. Most are confused by clocks with Roman numerals or other markings. Standardized test questions typically ascertain that first graders can tell time on analog clock faces with bold Arabic numerals, to the hour.

Elapsed Time

The concept of elapsed time confuses even many middle first graders. Most late first graders are able to solve simple problems with dates, whole hours, and whole minutes, but are unable to perform problems with hours that cross noon or midnight, or that span months on the calendar or more than one minute.

For example, your child will probably be able to understand that Thursday is three days later than Monday, but she may be confused by the fact that Monday is four days later than Thursday (because a new week has started since last Thursday). She will be able to understand that Susie began riding her bicycle to Grandma's at 10:10 and arrived at 10:30, so the trip took 20 minutes; but she may be unable to understand that Tommy began riding his bicycle to Grandpa's at 10:50 and arrived at 11:10, and that trip also took 20 minutes. She will be able to understand that the family left for vacation on August 2 and returned home on August 9, so the vacation lasted 7 days, but she may not understand that another family's vacation that began on July 27 and ended on August 3 also lasted 7 days (because a new month began during the vacation).

Standardized tests at first-grade level ascertain children's ability to understand simple elapsed time problems. Questions may give a time when an activity starts and when it stops, asking your child to figure out how much time has elapsed in between.

Bar Graphs and Pictographs

By late first grade, most children are able to understand simple graphical representations. For example, when they watch old war movies and see that the ace had pictures of 12 enemy fighters next to his cockpit, they know that signifies that he had shot down 12 enemy aircraft. Most are also able to understand simple bar charts.

Most first graders are not able to understand more sophisticated graphs and pictograms, such as the type of charts used in the stock market or pie charts. Their understanding is limited to simple, linear, one-to-one scale bar charts and pictograms.

Congruence and Symmetry

Early first graders can be quite inflexible in their thinking. Many will fail to recognize, for example, that a pound of feathers and a pound of lead weigh the same, although many late first graders will see the humor in such a comparison. Instead, many early first graders believe that when liquid is poured into a short, fat container and an identical amount is poured into a tall, slender one, the tall, slender container still contains more.

However, by late first grade your child will probably understand that the amount of liquid remains the same regardless of the shape of the container.

Many early first graders also fail to see that a shape flipped on its side or reversed is still the same shape, while many late first graders understand that the shape remains the same even if rotated.

Spatial Relations

Most late first graders are capable of understanding basic spatial relationships such as *above*, *below*, *beside*, and *behind*. Although some still confuse left and right, most understand these relationships as well.

Nonstandard Units of Measurement

We don't always have a ruler available when we need to measure length, and we don't always have other standard instruments available when we need to measure other things.

Most late first graders are able to understand that sometimes we can measure things with nonstandard units. Children at this age are frequently masters at improvisation. For example, if they are measuring a length of board they need to finish the door over a house they are building for the dog, they will be able to measure the length they need to find or cut by measuring hand widths or by marking the length on a stick or piece of string.

Standard and Metric Units of Measurement

Most first graders are able to make simple measurements with single inches, feet, ounces, and pounds, but most aren't able to measure in fractions, and most are unfamiliar with the metric system. (However, unfamiliarity with the metric system at this age is rapidly disappearing, as more first-grade curricula incorporate the metric system.)

Most first graders are able to make direct measurements but will be confused by indirect measurements and estimation. For example, if given a tape measure, they will be able to tell you that the dog is 21 inches long, but they will be unable to estimate the dog's length.

Practice Skill: Measurement

Directions: Choose the correct answers for the following questions.

> **3** Lisa and Jimmy need 3 feet of rope to tie the scarecrow to the post in their garden. What will they use to measure how much rope to cut?
>
> Ⓐ cash register
>
> Ⓑ bathroom scale
>
> Ⓒ measuring cup
>
> Ⓓ yardstick

APRIL 2000

Sunday	Monday	Tuesday	Wednesday	Thursday	Friday	Saturday
						1
2	3	4	5	6	7	8
9	10	(11)	12	13	14	15
16	17	18	19	20	21	22
23 30	24	25	26	27	28	29

6 What coins are in this picture?

Ⓐ a nickel, a dime, and a quarter

Ⓑ two nickels and one dime

Ⓒ two dimes and a nickel

Ⓓ a penny, a nickel, and a dime

4 What date is circled on the calendar above?

Ⓐ April 11

Ⓑ April 1

Ⓒ May 15

Ⓓ December 1

7 What time is it on the clock above?

Ⓐ 12:00

Ⓑ 9:00

Ⓒ 15:00

Ⓓ 12:15

5 On the calendar above, what day of the week is circled?

Ⓐ Monday

Ⓑ Wednesday

Ⓒ Saturday

Ⓓ Tuesday

8 Charlie left to play ball at 2:00 p.m. His mother told him to be home by 5:00 p.m. How many hours did Charlie get to play?

Ⓐ 7

Ⓑ 3

Ⓒ 4

Ⓓ 2

10 What does the picture above show?

Ⓐ The cat and the dog are on the box.

Ⓑ The cat and the dog are beside the box.

Ⓒ The dog is on the box, and the cat is beside the box.

Ⓓ The cat is on the box, and the dog is beside the box.

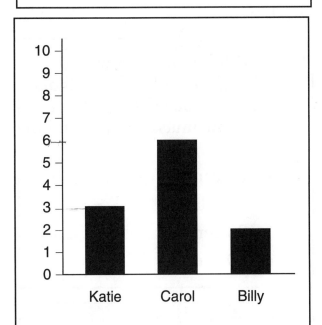

9 Look at the graph above. Katie, Carol, and Billy sold bars of candy. Katie sold 3 bars. How many bars did Carol sell?

Ⓐ 3

Ⓑ 2

Ⓒ 6

Ⓓ 10

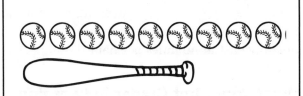

11 How many balls long is the bat in the picture above?

Ⓐ 6

Ⓑ 10

Ⓒ 3

Ⓓ 16

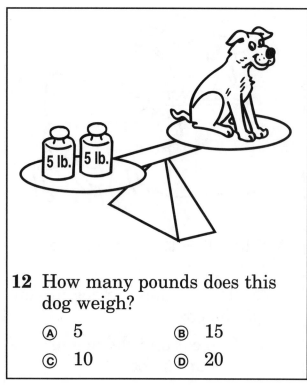

12 How many pounds does this dog weigh?

  Ⓐ 5   Ⓑ 15

  Ⓒ 10   Ⓓ 20

(See page 112 for answer key.)

Word Problems

Unfortunately, most people with math phobia in our culture are fearful of word problems. Even educated adults wince at the well-worn, "If one train is leaving the station heading north at 30 miles per hour and another leaves the station heading east at 40 miles per hour..."

What Your First Grader Is Learning

Most early first graders are able to answer simple, straightforward word problems involving whole units. For example, word problems that children this age may encounter include questions involving inches, feet, pounds, and ounces, without relying on fractions or regrouping.

What Tests May Ask

If word problems are too complex, with irrelevant elements thrown in to the questions, most first graders will be totally confused. Expect older students to be able to avoid such confusion, but realize that first graders are still susceptible. Standardized tests present word problems that are straightforward and not too confusing, such as the examples in the Practice Skill.

Practice Skill: Word and Oral Problems

Directions: Choose the correct answers for the following questions.

13 Terri found a quarter in the sofa cushions. Then she found a dime under the chair cushion. How much did she find in all?

  Ⓐ 35 cents

  Ⓑ 1 dollar

  Ⓒ 25 cents

  Ⓓ 10 cents

14 Jessica planted two bags of seeds in her garden on Monday, one bag of seeds on Tuesday, and three bags on Wednesday. How many bags of seeds did she plant in all?

  Ⓐ 8

  Ⓑ 6

  Ⓒ 7

  Ⓓ 9

15 Fiona had two baskets of Easter candy. One basket had five chocolate eggs and the other basket had three jelly beans and four marshmallow rabbits. How many pieces of candy did she have in all?

Ⓐ 5   Ⓑ 9

Ⓒ 11   Ⓓ 12

(See page 112 for answer key.)

Web Sites and Resources for More Information

Homework

Homework Central
http://www.HomeworkCentral.com
Terrific site for students, parents, and teachers, filled with information, projects, and more.

Win the Homework Wars
(Sylvan Learning Centers)
http://www.educate.com/online/qa_peters.html

Reading and Grammar Help

Born to Read: How to Raise a Reader
http://www.ala.org/alsc/raise_a_reader.html

Guide to Grammar and Writing
http://webster.commnet.edu/hp/pages/darling/grammar.htm
Help with "plague words and phrases," grammar FAQs, sentence parts, punctuation, rules for common usage.

Internet Public Library: Reading Zone
http://www.ipl.org/cgi-bin/youth/youth.out

Keeping Kids Reading and Writing
http://www.tiac.net/users/maryl/

U.S. Dept. of Education: Helping Your Child Learn to Read
http://www.ed.gov/pubs/parents/Reading/index.html

Math Help

Center for Advancement of Learning
http://www.muskingum.edu/%7Ecal/database/Math2.html
Substitution and memory strategies for math.

Center for Advancement of Learning
http://www.muskingum.edu/%7Ecal/database/Math1.html
General tips and suggestions.

Math.com
http://www.math.com
The world of math online.

Math.com
http://www.math.com/student/testprep.html
Get ready for standardized tests.

Math.com: Homework Help in Math
http://www.math.com/students/homework.html

Math.com: Math for Homeschoolers
http://www.math.com/parents/homeschool.html

The Math Forum: Problems and Puzzles
http://forum.swarthmore.edu/library/resource_types/problems_puzzles
Lots of fun math puzzles and problems for grades K through 12.

The Math Forum: Math Tips and Tricks
http://forum.swarthmore.edu/k12/mathtips/mathtips.html

Tips on Testing

Books on Test Preparation

http://www.testbooksonline.com/preHS.asp
This site provides printed resources for parents who wish to help their children prepare for standardized school tests.

Core Knowledge Web Site

http://www.coreknowledge.org/
Site dedicated to providing resources for parents; based on the books of E. D. Hirsch, Jr., who wrote the *What Your X Grader Needs to Know* series.

Family Education Network

http://www.familyeducation.com/article/0,1120,
1-6219,00.html
This report presents some of the arguments against current standardized testing practices in the public schools. The site also provides links to family activities that help kids learn.

Math.com

http://www.math.com/students/testprep.html
Get ready for standardized tests.

Standardized Tests

http://arc.missouri.edu/k12/
K through 12 assessment tools and know-how.

Parents: Testing in Schools

KidSource: Talking to Your Child's Teacher about Standardized Tests

http://www.kidsource.com/kidsource/content2/
talking.assessment.k12.4.html
This site provides basic information to help parents understand their children's test results and provides pointers for how to discuss the results with their children's teachers.

eSCORE.com: State Test and Education Standards

http://www.eSCORE.com
Find out if your child meets the necessary requirements for your local schools. A Web site with experts from Brazelton Institute and Harvard's Project Zero.

Overview of States' Assessment Programs

http://ericae.net/faqs/

Parent Soup
Education Central: Standardized Tests

http://www.parentsoup.com/edcentral/testing
A parent's guide to standardized testing in the schools, written from a parent advocacy standpoint.

National Center for Fair and Open Testing, Inc. (FairTest)

342 Broadway
Cambridge, MA 02139
(617) 864-4810
http://www.fairtest.org

National Parent Information Network

http://npin.org

Publications for Parents from the U.S. Department of Education

http://www.ed.gov/pubs/parents/
An ever-changing list of information for parents available from the U.S. Department of Education.

State of the States Report

http://www.edweek.org/sreports/qc99/states/
indicators/in-intro.htm
A report on testing and achievement in the 50 states.

Testing: General Information

Academic Center for Excellence

http://www.acekids.com

American Association for Higher Education Assessment

http://www.aahe.org/assessment/web.htm

American Educational Research Association (AERA)

http://aera.net
An excellent link to reports on American education, including reports on the controversy over standardized testing.

American Federation of Teachers

555 New Jersey Avenue, NW
Washington, D.C. 20011

Association of Test Publishers Member Products and Services
http://www.testpublishers.org/memserv.htm

Education Week on the Web
http://www.edweek.org

ERIC Clearinghouse on Assessment and Evaluation
1131 Shriver Lab
University of Maryland
College Park, MD 20742
http://ericae.net
A clearinghouse of information on assessment and education reform.

FairTest: The National Center for Fair and Open Testing
http://fairtest.org/facts/ntfact.htm
http://fairtest.org/
The National Center for Fair and Open Testing is an advocacy organization working to end the abuses, misuses, and flaws of standardized testing and to ensure that evaluation of students and workers is fair, open, and educationally sound. This site provides many links to fact sheets, opinion papers, and other sources of information about testing.

National Congress of Parents and Teachers
700 North Rush Street
Chicago, Illinois 60611

National Education Association
1201 16th Street, NW
Washington, DC 20036

National School Boards Association
http://www.nsba.org
A good source for information on all aspects of public education, including standardized testing.

Testing Our Children: A Report Card on State Assessment Systems
http://www.fairtest.org/states/survey.htm
Report of testing practices of the states, with graphical links to the states and a critique of fair testing practices in each state.

Trends in Statewide Student Assessment Programs: A Graphical Summary
http://www.ccsso.org/survey96.html
Results of annual survey of states' departments of public instruction regarding their testing practices.

U.S. Department of Education
http://www.ed.gov/

Web Links for Parents Who Want to Help Their Children Achieve
http://www.liveandlearn.com/learn.html
This page offers many Web links to free and for-sale information and materials for parents who want to help their children do well in school. Titles include such free offerings as the Online Colors Game and questionnaires to determine whether your child is ready for school.

What Should Parents Know about Standardized Testing in the Schools?
http://www.rusd.k12.ca.us/parents/standard.html
An online brochure about standardized testing in the schools, with advice regarding how to become an effective advocate for your child.

Test Publishers Online

ACT: Information for Life's Transitions
http://www.act.org

American Guidance Service, Inc.
http://www.agsnet.com

Ballard & Tighe Publishers
http://www.ballard-tighe.com

Consulting Psychologists Press
http://www.cpp-db.com

CTB McGraw-Hill
http://www.ctb.com

Educational Records Bureau
http://www.erbtest.org/index.html

Educational Testing Service
http://www.ets.org

General Educational Development (GED) Testing Service
http://www.acenet.edu/calec/ged/home.html

Harcourt Brace Educational Measurement
http://www.hbem.com

Piney Mountain Press—A Cyber-Center for Career and Applied Learning
http://www.pineymountain.com

ProEd Publishing
http://www.proedinc.com

Riverside Publishing Company
http://www.hmco.com/hmco/riverside

Stoelting Co.
http://www.stoeltingco.com

Sylvan Learning Systems, Inc.
http://www.educate.com

Touchstone Applied Science Associates, Inc. (TASA)
http://www.tasa.com

Tests Online

(*Note:* We don't endorse tests; some may not have technical documentation. Evaluate the quality of any testing program before making decisions based on its use.)

Edutest, Inc.
http://www.edutest.com
Edutest is an Internet-accessible testing service that offers criterion-referenced tests for elementary school students, based upon the standards for K through 12 learning and achievement in the states of Virginia, California, and Florida.

Virtual Knowledge
http://www.smarterkids.com
This commercial service, which enjoys a formal partnership with Sylvan Learning Centers, offers a line of skills assessments for preschool through grade 9 for use in the classroom or the home. For free online sample tests, see the Virtual Test Center.

Read More about It

Abbamont, Gary W. *Test Smart: Ready-to-Use Test-Taking Strategies and Activities for Grades 5–12. Upper Saddle River,* NJ: Prentice Hall Direct, 1997.

Cookson, Peter W., and Joshua Halberstam. *A Parent's Guide to Standardized Tests in School: How to Improve Your Child's Chances for Success.* New York: Learning Express, 1998.

Frank, Steven, and Stephen Frank. *Test-Taking Secrets: Study Better, Test Smarter, and Get Great Grades (The Backpack Study Series).* Holbrook, MA: Adams Media Corporation, 1998.

Gilbert, Sara Dulaney. *How to Do Your Best on Tests: A Survival Guide.* New York: Beech Tree Books, 1998.

Gruber, Gary. *Dr. Gary Gruber's Essential Guide to Test-Taking for Kids, Grades 3–5.* New York: William Morrow & Co., 1986.

———. *Gary Gruber's Essential Guide to Test-Taking for Kids, Grades 6, 7, 8, 9.* New York: William Morrow & Co., 1997.

Leonhardt, Mary. *99 Ways to Get Kids to Love Reading and 100 Books They'll Love.* New York: Crown, 1997.

———. *Parents Who Love Reading, Kids Who Don't: How It Happens and What You Can Do about It.* New York: Crown, 1995.

McGrath, Barbara B. *The Baseball Counting Book.* Watertown, MA: Charlesbridge, 1999.

———. *More M&M's Brand Chocolate Candies Math.* Watertown, MA: Charlesbridge, 1998.

Mokros, Janice R. *Beyond Facts & Flashcards: Exploring Math with Your Kids.* Portsmouth, NH: Heinemann, 1996.

Romain, Trevor, and Elizabeth Verdick. *True or False?: Tests Stink!* Minneapolis: Free Spirit Publishing Co., 1999.

Schartz, Eugene M. *How to Double Your Child's Grades in School: Build Brilliance and Leadership into Your Child—from Kindergarten to College—in Just 5 Minutes a Day.* New York: Barnes & Noble, 1999.

Taylor, Kathe, and Sherry Walton. *Children at the Center: A Workshop Approach to Standardized Test Preparation, K–8.* Portsmouth, NH: Heinemann, 1998.

Tobia, Sheila. *Overcoming Math Anxiety.* New York: W. W. Norton & Company, Inc., 1995.

Tufariello, Ann Hunt. *Up Your Grades: Proven Strategies for Academic Success.* Lincolnwood, IL: VGM Career Horizons, 1996.

Vorderman, Carol. *How Math Works.* Pleasantville, NY: Reader's Digest Association, Inc., 1996.

Zahler, Kathy A. *50 Simple Things You Can Do to Raise a Child Who Loves to Read.* New York: IDG Books, 1997.

What Your Child's Test Scores Mean

Several weeks or months after your child has taken standardized tests, you will receive a report such as the TerraNova Home Report found in Figures 1 and 2. You will receive similar reports if your child has taken other tests. We briefly examine what information the reports include.

Look at the first page of the Home Report. Note that the chart provides labeled bars showing the child's performance. Each bar is labeled with the child's National Percentile for that skill area. When you know how to interpret them, national percentiles can be the most useful scores you encounter on reports such as this. Even when you are confronted with different tests that use different scale scores, you can always interpret percentiles the same way, regardless of the test. A percentile tells the percent of students who score at or below that level. A percentile of 25, for example, means that 25 percent of children taking the test scored at or below that score. (It also means that 75 percent of students scored above that score.) Note that the average is always at the 50th percentile.

On the right side of the graph on the first page of the report, the publisher has designated the ranges of scores that constitute average, above average, and below average. You can also use this slightly more precise key for interpreting percentiles:

PERCENTILE RANGE	LEVEL
2 and Below	Deficient
3–8	Borderline
9–23	Low Average
24–75	Average
76–97	High Average
98 and Up	Superior

The second page of the Home report provides a listing of the child's strengths and weaknesses, along with keys for mastery, partial mastery, and non-mastery of the skills. Scoring services determine these breakdowns based on the child's scores as compared with those from the national norm group.

Your child's teacher or guidance counselor will probably also receive a profile report similar to the TerraNova Individual Profile Report, shown in Figures 3 and 4. That report will be kept in your child's permanent record. The first aspect of this report to notice is that the scores are expressed both numerically and graphically.

First look at the score bands under National Percentile. Note that the scores are expressed as bands, with the actual score represented by a dot within each band. The reason we express the scores as bands is to provide an idea of the amount by which typical scores may vary for each student. That is, each band represents a

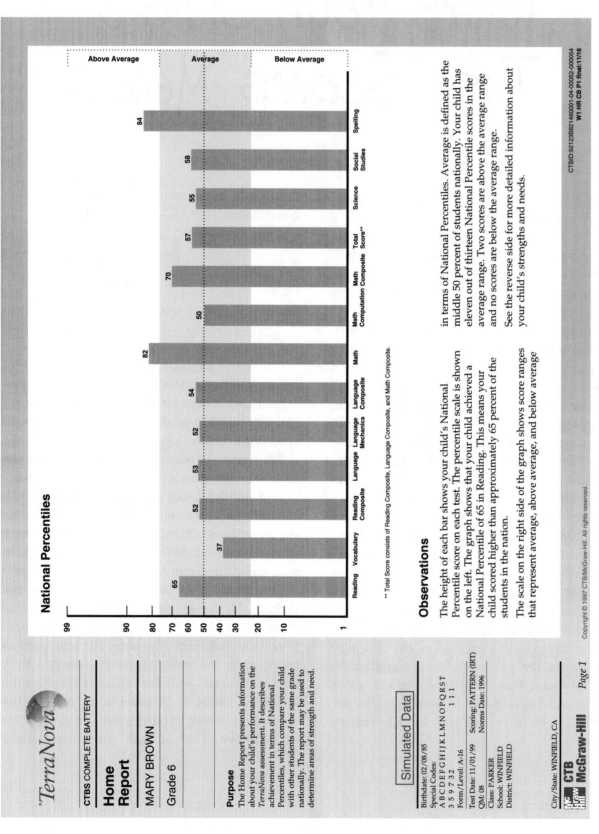

Figure 1 (SOURCE: CTB/McGraw-Hill, copyright © 1997. All rights reserved. Reproduced with permission.)

TerraNova

CTBS COMPLETE BATTERY

Home Report

MARY BROWN

Grade 6

Purpose

This page of the Home Report presents information about your child's strengths and needs. This information is provided to help you monitor your child's academic growth.

Simulated Data

Birthdate: 02/08/85
Special Codes:
A B C D E F G H I J K L M N O P Q R S T
3 5 9 7 3 2   1 1 1
Form/Level: A-16
Test Date: 11/01/99   Scoring: PATTERN (IRT)
QM: 08   Norms Date: 1996

Class: PARKER
School: WINFIELD
District: WINFIELD

City/State: WINFIELD, CA

CTB/McGraw-Hill   *Page 2*   Copyright © 1997 CTB/McGraw-Hill. All rights reserved.

Strengths

Reading
● Basic Understanding
● Analyze Text

Vocabulary
● Word Meaning
● Words in Context

Language
● Editing Skills
● Sentence Structure

Language Mechanics
● Sentences, Phrases, Clauses

Mathematics
● Computation and Numerical Estimation
● Operation Concepts

Mathematics Computation
● Add Whole Numbers
● Multiply Whole Numbers

Science
● Life Science
● Inquiry Skills

Social Studies
● Geographic Perspectives
● Economic Perspectives

Spelling
● Vowels
● Consonants

Key ● Mastery

General Interpretation

The left column shows your child's best areas of performance. In each case, your child has reached mastery level. The column at the right shows the areas within each test section where your child's scores are the lowest. In these cases, your child has not reached mastery level, although he or she may have reached partial mastery.

Needs

Reading
◖ Evaluate and Extend Meaning
○ Identify Reading Strategies

Vocabulary
○ Multimeaning Words

Language
◖ Writing Strategies

Language Mechanics
○ Writing Conventions

Mathematics
◖ Measurement
◖ Geometry and Spatial Sense

Mathematics Computation
○ Percents

Science
○ Earth and Space Science

Social Studies
◖ Historical and Cultural Perspectives

Spelling
No area of needs were identified for this content area

Key ◖ Partial Mastery   ○ Non-Mastery

Figure 2 (SOURCE: CTB/McGraw-Hill, copyright © 1997. All rights reserved. Reproduced with permission.)

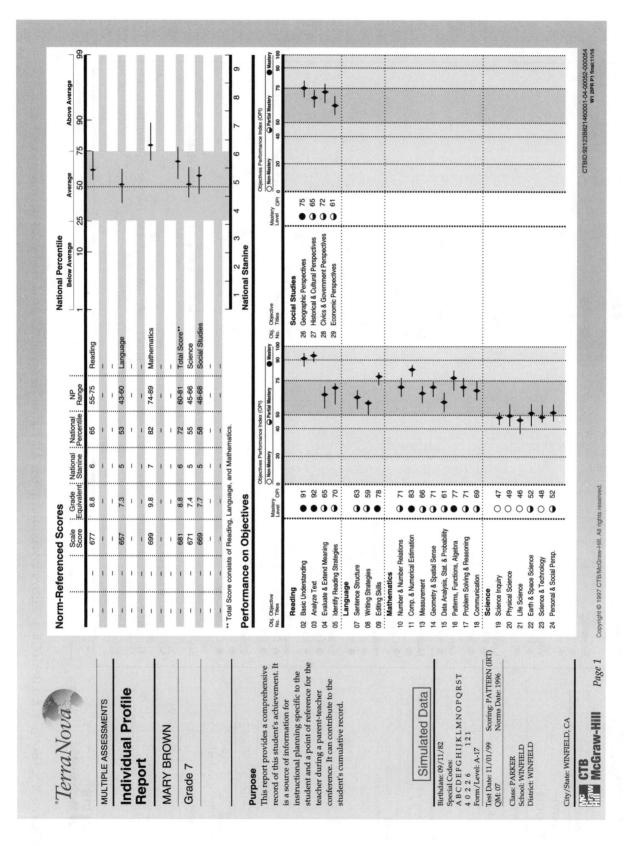

Figure 3 (SOURCE: CTB/McGraw-Hill, copyright © 1997. All rights reserved. Reproduced with permission.)

Observations

Norm-Referenced Scores

The top section of the report presents information about this student's achievement in several different ways. The National Percentile (NP) data and graph indicate how this student performed compared to students of the same grade nationally. The National Percentile range indicates that if this student had taken the test numerous times the scores would have fallen within the range shown. The shaded area on the graph represents the average range of scores, usually defined as the middle 50 percent of students nationally. Scores in the area to the right of the shading are above the average range. Scores in the area to the left of the shading are below the average range.

In Reading, for example, this student achieved a National Percentile rank of 65. This student scored higher than 65 percent of the students nationally. This score is in the average range. This student has a total of five scores in the average range. One score is in the above average range. No scores are in the below average range.

Performance on Objectives

The next section of the report presents performance on the objectives. Each objective is measured by a minimum of 4 items. The Objectives Performance Index (OPI) provides an estimate of the number of items that a student could be expected to answer correctly if there had been 100 items for that objective. The OPI is used to indicate mastery of each objective. An OPI of 75 and above characterizes Mastery. An OPI between 50 and 74 indicates Partial Mastery, and an OPI below 50 indicates Non-Mastery. The two-digit number preceding the objective title identifies the objective, which is fully described in the Teacher's Guide to *TerraNova*. The bands on either side of the diamonds indicate the range within which the student's test scores would fall if the student were tested numerous times.

In Reading, for example, this student could be expected to respond correctly to 91 out of 100 items measuring Basic Understanding. If this student had taken the test numerous times the OPI for this objective would have fallen between 82 and 93.

Teacher Notes

TerraNova

MULTIPLE ASSESSMENTS

Individual Profile Report

MARY BROWN

Grade 7

Purpose

The Observations section of the Individual Profile Report gives teachers and parents information to interpret this report. This page is a narrative description of the data on the other side.

Simulated Data

Birthdate: 09/11/82
Special Codes:
A B C D E F G H I J K L M N O P Q R S T
4 0 2 2 6   1 2 1
Form/Level: A-17
Test Date: 11/01/99   Scoring: PATTERN (IRT)
QM: 08   Norms Date: 1996

Class: PARKER
School: WINFIELD
District: WINFIELD

City/State: WINFIELD, CA

CTB McGraw-Hill   *Page 2*   Copyright © 1997 CTB/McGraw-Hill. All rights reserved.

Figure 4 (SOURCE: CTB/McGraw-Hill, copyright © 1997. All rights reserved. Reproduced with permission.)

TerraNova

MULTIPLE ASSESSMENTS

Student Performance Level Report

KEN ALLEN

Grade 4

Purpose

This report describes this student's achievement in terms of five performance levels for each content area. The meaning of these levels is described on the back of this page. Performance levels are a new way of describing achievement.

| Simulated Data |

Birthdate: 02/08/86
Special Codes:
A B C D E F G H I J K L M N O P Q R S T
3 5 9 7 3 2   1 1 1
Form/Level: A-14

Test Date: 04/15/97   Scoring: PATTERN (IRT)
QM: 31   Norms Date: 1996

Class: SCHWARZ
School: WINFIELD
District: GREEN VALLEY

City/State: WINFIELD, CA

CTB
McGraw-Hill   *Page 1*

Performance Levels	Reading	Language	Mathematics	Science	Social Studies
5 Advanced					
4 Proficient					
3 Nearing Proficiency	✓				✓
2 Progressing	✓	✓	✓	✓	✓
1 Step 1	✓	✓	✓	✓	✓

Partially Proficient

Observations

Performance level scores provide a measure of what students *can do* in terms of the content and skills assessed by *TerraNova*, and typically found in curricula for Grades 3, 4, and 5. It is desirable to work towards achieving a Level 4 (Proficient) or Level 5 (Advanced) by the end of Grade 5.

The number of check marks indicates the performance level this student reached in each content area. For example, this student reached Level 3 in Reading and Social Studies.

The performance level indicates this student can perform the majority of what is described for that level and even more of what is described for the levels below. The student may also be capable of performing some of the things described in the next higher level, but not enough to have reached that level of performance.

For example, this student can perform the majority of what is described for Level 3 in Reading and even more of what is described for Level 2 and Level 1 in Reading. This student may also be capable of performing some of what is described for Level 4 in Reading.

For each content area look at the skills and knowledge described in the next higher level. These are the competencies this student needs to demonstrate to show academic growth.

Figure 5 (SOURCE: CTB/McGraw-Hill, copyright © 1997. All rights reserved. Reproduced with permission.)

Performance Levels (Grades 3, 4, 5)	Reading	Language	Mathematics	Science	Social Studies
5 Advanced	Students use analogies to generalize. They identify a paraphrase of concepts or ideas in texts. They can indicate thought processes that led them to a previous answer. In written responses, they demonstrate understanding of an implied theme, assess intent of passage information, and provide justification as well as support for their answers.	Students understand logical development in paragraph structure. They identify essential information from notes. They recognize the effect of prepositional phrases on subject-verb agreement. They find and correct at least 4 out of 6 errors when editing simple narratives. They correct run-on and incomplete sentences in more complex texts. They can eliminate all errors when editing their own work.	Students locate decimals on a number line; compute with decimals and fractions; read scale drawings; find areas; identify geometric transformations; construct and label bar graphs; find simple probabilities; find averages; use patterns in data to solve problems; use multiple strategies and concepts to solve unfamiliar problems; express mathematical ideas and explain the problem-solving process.	Students understand a broad range of grade level scientific concepts, such as the structure of Earth and instinctive behavior. They know terminology, such as decomposers, fossil fuel, eclipse, and buoyancy. Knowledge of more complex environmental issues includes, for example, the positive consequences of a forest fire. Students can process and interpret more detailed tables and graphs. They can suggest improvements to experimental design, such as running more trials.	Students consistently demonstrate skills such as synthesizing information from two sources (e.g., a document and a map). They show understanding of the democratic process and global environmental issues, and know the location of continents and major countries. They analyze and summarize information from multiple sources in early American history. They thoroughly explain both sides of an issue and give complete and detailed written answers to questions.
4 Proficient	Students interpret figures of speech. They recognize paraphrase of information and retrieve information to complete forms. In more complex texts, they identify themes, main ideas, or author purpose/point of view. They analyze and apply information in graphic and text form, make reasonable generalizations, and draw conclusions. In written responses, they can identify key elements from text.	Students select the best supporting sentences for a topic sentence. They use compound predicates to combine sentences. They identify simple subjects and predicates, recognize correct usage when confronted with two types of errors, and find and correct at least 3 out of 6 errors when editing simple narratives. They can edit their own work with only minor errors.	Students compare, order, and round whole numbers; know place value to thousands; identify fractions; use computation and estimation strategies; relate multiplication to addition; measure to nearest half-inch and centimeter; measure and find perimeters; estimate measures; find elapsed times; combine and subdivide shapes; identify parallel lines; interpret tables and graphs; solve two-step problems.	Students have a range of specific science knowledge, including details about animal adaptations and classification, states of matter, and the geology of Earth. They recognize scientific words such as habitat, gravity, and mass. They understand the usefulness of computers. They understand reasons for conserving natural resources. Understanding of experimentation includes analyzing purpose, interpreting data, and selecting tools to gather data.	Students demonstrate skills such as making inferences, using historical documents and analyzing maps to determine the economic strengths of a region. They understand the function of currency in various cultures and supply and demand. They summarize information from multiple sources, recognize relationships, determine relevance of information, and show global awareness. They propose solutions to real-world problems and support ideas with appropriate details.
3 Nearing Proficiency	Students use context clues and structural analysis to determine word meaning. They recognize homonyms and antonyms in grade-level text. They identify important details, sequence, cause and effect, and lessons embedded in the text. They interpret characters' feelings and apply information to new situations. In written responses, they can express an opinion and support it.	Students identify irrelevant sentences in paragraphs and select the best place to insert new information. They recognize faulty sentence construction. They can combine simple sentences with conjunctions and use simple subordination of phrases/clauses. They identify reference sources. They recognize correct conventions for dates, closings, and place names in informal correspondence.	Students identify even and odd numbers; subtract whole numbers with regrouping; multiply and divide by one-digit numbers; identify simple fractions; measure with ruler to nearest inch; tell time to nearest fifteen minutes; recognize and classify common shapes; recognize symmetry; subdivide shapes; complete bar graphs; extend numerical and geometric patterns; apply simple logical reasoning.	Students are familiar with the life cycles of plants and animals. They can identify an example of a cold-blooded animal. They infer what once existed from fossil evidence. They understand the water cycle. They know science and society issues such as recycling and sources of pollution. They can sequence technological advances. They extrapolate data, devise a simple classification scheme, and determine the purpose of a simple experiment.	Students demonstrate skills in organizing information. They use time lines, product and global maps, and cardinal directions. They understand simple cause and effect relationships and historical documents. They sequence events, associate holidays with events, and classify natural resources. They compare life in different times and understand some economic concepts related to products, jobs, and the environment. They give some detail in written responses.
2 Progressing	Students identify synonyms for grade-level words, and use context clues to define common words. They make simple inferences and predictions based on text. They identify characters' feelings. They can transfer information from text to graphic form, or from graphic form to text. In written responses, they can provide limited support for their answers.	Students identify the use of correct verb tenses and supply verbs to complete sentences. They complete paragraphs by selecting an appropriate topic sentence. They select correct adjective forms.	Students know ordinal numbers; solve coin combination problems; count by tens; add whole numbers with regrouping; have basic estimation skills; understand addition property of zero; write and identify number sentences describing simple situations; read calendars; identify appropriate measurement tools; use simple coordinate grids; read common tables and graphs.	Students recognize that plants decompose and become part of soil. They can classify a plant as a vegetable. They recognize that camouflage relates to survival. They recognize terms such as hibernate. They have an understanding of human impact on the environment and are familiar with causes of pollution. They find the correct bar graph to represent given data and transfer data appropriate for middle elementary grades to a bar graph.	Students demonstrate simple information-processing skills such as using basic maps and keys. They recognize simple geographical terms, types of jobs, modes of transportation, and natural resources. They connect a human need with an appropriate community service. They identify some early famous presidents and know the capital of the United States. Their written answers are partially complete.
1 Step 1	Students select pictured representations of ideas and identify stated details contained in simple texts. In written responses, they can select and transfer information from charts.	Students supply subjects to complete sentences. They identify the correct use of pronouns. They edit for the correct use of end marks and initial capital letters, and identify the correct convention for greetings in letters.	Students read and recognize numbers to 1000; identify real-world use of numbers; add and subtract two-digit numbers without regrouping; identify addition situations; recognize and complete simple geometric and numerical patterns.	Students recognize basic animal adaptations for living in the water, identify an animal that is hatched from an egg, and associate an organism with its correct environment. They identify an object as metal. They have some understanding of conditions on the moon. They supply one way a computer can be useful. They associate an instrument like a telescope with a field of study.	Students are developing fundamental social studies skills such as locating and classifying basic information. They locate information in pictures and read and complete simple bar graphs related to social studies concepts and contexts. They can connect some city buildings with their functions and recognize certain historical objects.

Partially Proficient (bracket label spanning levels 3, 2, 1)

W1 SPLR P2:11/02

IMPORTANT: Each performance level, depicted on the other side, indicates the student can perform the majority of what is described for that level and even more of what is described for the levels below. The student may also be capable of performing some of the things described in the next higher level, but not enough to have reached that level.

Figure 6

confidence interval. In these reports, we usually report either a 90 percent or 95 percent confidence interval. Interpret a confidence interval this way: Suppose we report a 90 percent confidence interval of 25 to 37. This means we estimate that, if the child took the test multiple times, we would expect that child's score to be in the 25 to 37 range 90 percent of the time.

Now look under the section titled Norm-Referenced Scores on the first page of the Individual Profile Report (Figure 3). The farthest column on the right provides the NP Range, which is the National Percentile scores represented by the score bands in the chart.

Next notice the column labeled Grade Equivalent. Theoretically, grade level equivalents equate a student's score in a skill area with the average grade placement of children who made the same score. Many psychologists and test developers would prefer that we stopped reporting grade equivalents, because they can be grossly misleading. For example, the average reading grade level of high school seniors as reported by one of the more popular tests is the eighth grade level. Does that mean that the nation's high school seniors cannot read? No. The way the test publisher calculated grade equivalents was to determine the average test scores for students in grades 4 to 6 and then simply extend the resulting prediction formula to grades 7 to 12. The result is that parents of average high school seniors who take the test in question would mistakenly believe that their seniors are reading four grade levels behind! Stick to the percentile in interpreting your child's scores.

Now look at the columns labeled Scale Score and National Stanine. These are two of a group of scores we also call *standard scores.* In reports for other tests, you may see other standard scores reported, such as Normal Curve Equivalents (NCEs), Z-Scores, and T-Scores. The IQ that we report on intelligence tests, for example, is a standard score. Standard scores are simply a way of expressing a student's scores in terms of the statistical properties of the scores from the norm group against which we are comparing the child. Although most psychologists prefer to speak in terms of standard scores among themselves, parents are advised to stick to percentiles in interpreting your child's performance.

Now look at the section of the report labeled Performance on Objectives. In this section, the test publisher reports how your child did on the various skills that make up each skills area. Note that the scores on each objective are expressed as a percentile band, and you are again told whether your child's score constitutes mastery, non-mastery, or partial mastery. Note that these scores are made up of tallies of sometimes small numbers of test items taken from sections such as Reading or Math. Because they are calculated from a much smaller number of scores than the main scales are (for example, Sentence Comprehension is made up of fewer items than overall Reading), their scores are less reliable than those of the main scales.

Now look at the second page of the Individual Profile Report (Figure 4). Here the test publisher provides a narrative summary of how the child did on the test. These summaries are computer-generated according to rules provided by the publisher. Note that the results descriptions are more general than those on the previous three report pages. But they allow the teacher to form a general picture of which students are performing at what general skill levels.

Finally, your child's guidance counselor may receive a summary report such as the TerraNova Student Performance Level Report. (See Figures 5 and 6.) In this report, the publisher explains to school personnel what skills the test assessed and generally how proficiently the child tested under each skill.

Which States Require Which Tests

Tables 1 through 3 summarize standardized testing practices in the 50 states and the District of Columbia. This information is constantly changing; the information presented here was accurate as of the date of printing of this book. Many states have changed their testing practices in response to revised accountability legislation, while others have changed the tests they use.

Table 1 State Web Sites: Education and Testing

STATE	GENERAL WEB SITE	STATE TESTING WEB SITE
Alabama	http://www.alsde.edu/	http://www.fairtest.org/states/al.htm
Alaska	www.educ.state.ak.us/	http://www.eed.state.ak.us/tls/Performance Standards/
Arizona	http://www.ade.state.az.us/	http://www.ade.state.az.us/standards/
Arkansas	http://arkedu.k12.ar.us/	http://www.fairtest.org/states/ar.htm
California	http://goldmine.cde.ca.gov/	http://ww.cde.ca.gov/cilbranch/sca/
Colorado	http://www.cde.state.co.us/index_home.htm	http://www.cde.state.co.us/index_assess.htm
Connecticut	http://www.state.ct.us/sde	http://www.state.ct.us/sde/cmt/index.htm
Delaware	http://www.doe.state.de.us/	http://www.doe.state.de.us/aab/index.htm
District of Columbia	http://www.k12.dc.us/dcps/home.html	http://www.k12.dc.us/dcps/data/data_frame2.html
Florida	http://www.firn.edu/doe/	http://www.firn.edu/doe/sas/sasshome.htm
Georgia	http://www.doe.k12.ga.us/	http://www.doe.k12.ga.us/sla/ret/recotest.html
Hawaii	http://kalama.doe.hawaii.edu/upena/	http://www.fairtest.org/states/hi.htm
Idaho	http://www.sde.state.id.us/Dept/	http://www.sde.state.id.us/instruct/ schoolaccount/statetesting.htm
Illinois	http://www.isbe.state.il.us/	http://www.isbe.state.il.us/isat/
Indiana	http://doe.state.in.us/	http://doe.state.in.us/assessment/welcome.html
Iowa	http://www.state.ia.us/educate/index.html	(Tests Chosen Locally)
Kansas	http://www.ksbe.state.ks.us/	http://www.ksbe.state.ks.us/assessment/
Kentucky	htp://www.kde.state.ky.us/	http://www.kde.state.ky.us/oaa/
Louisiana	http://www.doe.state.la.us/DOE/asps/home.asp	http://www.doe.state.la.us/DOE/asps/home.asp? I=HISTAKES
Maine	http://janus.state.me.us/education/homepage.htm	http://janus.state.me.us/education/mea/ meacompass.htm
Maryland	http://www.msde.state.md.us/	http://www.fairtest.org/states/md.htm
Massachusetts	http://www.doe.mass.edu/	http://www.doe.mass.edu/mcas/
Michigan	http://www.mde.state.mi.us/	http://www.mde.state.mi.us/off/meap/

STATE	GENERAL WEB SITE	STATE TESTING WEB SITE
Minnesota	http://www.educ.state.mn.us/	http://fairtest.org/states/mn.htm
Mississippi	http://mdek12.state.ms.us/	http://fairtest.org/states/ms.htm
Missouri	http://services.dese.state.mo.us/	http://fairtest.org/states/mo.htm
Montana	http://www.metnet.mt.gov/	http://fairtest.org/states/mt.htm
Nebraska	http://nde4.nde.state.ne.us/	http://www.edneb.org/IPS/AppAccrd/ ApprAccrd.html
Nevada	http://www.nsn.k12.nv.us/nvdoe/	http://www.nsn.k12.nv.us/nvdoe/reports/ TerraNova.doc
New Hampshire	http://www.state.nh.us/doe/	http://www.state.nh.us/doe/Assessment/ assessme(NHEIAP).htm
New Jersey	http://ww.state.nj.us/education/	http://www.state.nj.us/njded/stass/index.html
New Mexico	http://sde.state.nm.us/	http://sde.state.nm.us/press/august30a.html
New York	http://www.nysed.gov/	http://www.emsc.nysed.gov/ciai/assess.html
North Carolina	http://www.dpi.state.nc.us/	http://www.dpi.state.nc.us/accountability/ reporting/index.html
North Dakota	http://www.dpi.state.nd.us/dpi/index.htm	http://www.dpi.state.nd.us/dpi/reports/ assess/assess.htm
Ohio	http://www.ode.state.oh.us/	http://www.ode.state.oh.us/ca/
Oklahoma	http://sde.state.ok.us/	http://sde.state.ok.us/acrob/testpack.pdf
Oregon	http://www.ode.state.or.us//	http://www.ode.state.or.us/assmt/index.htm
Pennsylvania	http://www.pde.psu.edu/ http://instruct.ride.ri.net/ride_home_page.html	http://www.fairtest.org/states/pa.htm
Rhode Island		
South Carolina	http://www.state.sc.us/sde/	http://www.state.sc.us/sde/reports/terranov.htm
South Dakota	http://www.state.sd.us/state/executive/deca/	http://www.state.sd.us/state/executive/deca/TA/ McRelReport/McRelReports.htm
Tennessee	http://www.state.tn.us/education/	http://www.state.tn.us/education/tsintro.htm
Texas	http://www.tea.state.tx.us/	http://www.tea.state.tx.us/student.assessment/
Utah	http://www.usoe.k12.ut.us/	http://www.usoe.k12.ut.us/eval.usoeeval.htm
Vermont	http://www.cit.state.vt.us/educ/	http://www.fairtest.org/states/vt.htm

STATE	GENERAL WEB SITE	STATE TESTING WEB SITE
Virginia	http://www.pen.k12.va.us/Anthology/VDOE/	http://www.pen.k12.va.us/VDOE/Assessment/home.shtml
Washington	http://www.k12.wa.us/	http://assessment.ospi.wednet.edu/
West Virginia	http://wvde.state.wv.us/	http://www.fairtest.org/states/wv.htm
Wisconsin	http://www.dpi.state.wi.us/	http://www.dpi.state.wi.us/dpi/oea/spr_kce.html
Wyoming	http://www.k12.wy.us/wdehome.html	http://www.asme.com/wycas/index.htm

Table 2   Norm-Referenced and Criterion-Referenced Tests Administered by State

STATE	NORM-REFERENCED TEST	CRITERION-REFERENCED TEST	EXIT EXAM
Alabama	Stanford Achievement Test		Alabama High School Graduation Exam
Alaska	California Achievement Test		
Arizona	Stanford Achievement Test	Arizona's Instrument to Measure Standards (AIMS)	
Arkansas	Stanford Achievement Test		
California	Stanford Achievement Test	Standardized Testing and Reporting Supplement	High School Exit Exam (HSEE)
Colorado	None	Colorado Student Assessment Program	
Connecticut		Connecticut Mastery Test	
Delaware	Stanford Achievement Test	Delaware Student Testing Program	
District of Columbia	Stanford Achievement Test		
Florida	(Locally Selected)	Florida Comprehensive Assessment Test (FCAT)	High School Competency Test (HSCT)
Georgia	Iowa Tests of Basic Skills	Criterion-Referenced Competency Tests (CRCT)	Georgia High School Graduation Tests
Hawaii	Stanford Achievement Test	Credit by Examination	Hawaii State Test of Essential Competencies
Idaho	Iowa Test of Basic Skills/ Tests of Direct Achievement and Proficiency	Writing/Mathematics Assessment	
Illinois		Illinois Standards Achievement Tests	Prairie State Achievement Examination
Indiana		Indiana Statewide Testing for Education Progress	
Iowa	(None)		
Kansas		(State-Developed Tests)	
Kentucky	Comprehensive Tests of Basic Skills	Kentucky Instructional Results Information System	
Louisiana	Iowa Tests of Basic Skills	Louisiana Educational Assessment Program	Graduate Exit Exam
Maine		Maine Educational Assessment	
Maryland		Maryland School Performance Assessment Program	
Massachusetts		Massachusetts Comprehensive Assessment System	

STATE	NORM-REFERENCED TEST	CRITERION-REFERENCED TEST	EXIT EXAM
Michigan		Michigan Educational Assessment Program	High School Test
Minnesota		Basic Standards Test	Profile of Learning
Mississippi	Iowa Test of Basic Skills	Subject Area Testing Program	Functional Literacy Examination
Missouri		Missouri Mastery and Achievement Test	
Montana	(districts' choice)		
Nebraska			
Nevada	TerraNova		Nevada High School Proficiency Examination
New Hampshire		NH Educational Improvement and Assessment Program	
New Jersey		Elementary School Proficiency Test/Early Warning Test	High School Proficiency Test
New Mexico	TerraNova		New Mexico High School Competency Exam
New York		Pupil Evaluation Program/ Preliminary Competency Test	Regents Competency Tests
North Carolina	Iowa Test of Basic Skills	NC End of Grade Test	
North Dakota	TerraNova	ND Reading, Writing Speaking, Listening, Math Test	
Ohio		Ohio Proficiency Tests	Ohio Proficiency Tests
Oklahoma	Iowa Tests of Basic Skills	Oklahoma Criterion-Referenced Tests	
Oregon		Oregon Statewide Assessment	
Pennsylvania		Pennsylvania System of School Assessment	
Rhode Island	Metropolitan Achievement Test		
South Carolina	TerraNova	Palmetto Achievement Challenge Tests	High School Exit Exam
South Dakota	Stanford Achievement Test		
Tennessee	Tennessee Comprehensive Assessment Program	Tennessee Comprehensive Assessment Program	
Texas		Texas Assessment of Academic Skills	Texas Assessment of Academic Skills
Utah	Stanford Achievement Test	Core Curriculum Testing	

STATE	NORM-REFERENCED TEST	CRITERION-REFERENCED TEST	EXIT EXAM
Vermont		New Standards Reference Exams	
Virginia	Stanford Achievement Test	Virginia Standards of Learning	Virginia Standards of Learning
Washington	Iowa Tests of Basic Skills	Washington Assessment of Student Learning	Washington Assessment of Student Learning
West Virginia	Stanford Achievement Test		
Wisconsin	TerraNova	Wisconsin Knowledge and Concepts Examinations	
Wyoming	TerraNova	Wyoming Comprehensive Assessment System	Wyoming Comprehensive Assessment System

Table 3   Standardized Test Schedules by State

STATE	KG	1	2	3	4	5	6	7	8	9	10	11	12	COMMENT
Alabama				X	X	X	X	X	X	X	X	X	X	
Alaska					X				X		X			
Arizona			X	X	X	X	X	X	X	X	X	X	X	
Arkansas					X	X		X	X		X	X	X	
California			X	X	X	X	X	X	X	X	X	X		
Colorado				X	X			X						
Connecticut					X		X		X					
Delaware				X	X	X			X		X	X		
District of Columbia		X	X	X	X	X	X	X	X	X	X	X		
Florida		X	X	X	X	X	X	X	X	X	X	X	X	There is no state-mandated norm-referenced testing. However, the state collects information furnished by local districts that elect to perform norm-referenced testing. The FCAT is administered to Grades 4, 8, and 10 to assess reading and Grades 5, 8, and 10 to assess math.
Georgia				X		X			X					
Hawaii				X			X		X		X			The Credit by Examination is voluntary and is given in Grade 8 in Algebra and Foreign Languages.
Idaho				X	X	X	X	X	X	X	X	X		
Illinois				X	X		X	X	X		X	X		Exit Exam failure will not disqualify students from graduation if all other requirements are met.
Indiana				X			X		X		X			
Iowa		*	*	*	*	*	*	*	*	*	*	*	*	*Iowa does not currently have a statewide testing program. Locally chosen assessments are administered to grades determined locally.
Kansas				X	X	X		X	X		X			

STATE	KG	1	2	3	4	5	6	7	8	9	10	11	12	COMMENT
Kentucky					X	X		X	X			X	X	
Louisiana				X		X	X	X		X				
Maine					X				X			X		
Maryland				X		X			X					
Massachusetts					X				X		X			
Michigan					X	X		X	X					
Minnesota				X		X			X					Testing Information from Fair Test.Org. There was no readily accessible state-sponsored site.
Mississippi					X	X	X	X	X					State's Web site refused connection; all data were obtained from FairTest.Org.
Missouri			X	X	X	X	X	X	X	X	X			
Montana					X				X		X			The State Board of Education has decided to use a single norm-referenced test statewide beginning 2000–2001 school year.
Nebraska		**	**	**	**	**	**	**	**	**	**	**	**	**Decisions regarding testing are left to the individual school districts.
Nevada					X				X					Districts choose whether and how to test with norm-referenced tests.
New Hampshire				X			X				X			
New Jersey				X	X			X	X	X	X	X		
New Mexico					X		X		X					
New York					X				X	X				Assessment program is going through major revisions.
North Carolina				X	X	X	X	X	X		X			NRT Testing selects samples of students, not all.
North Dakota					X		X		X		X			
Ohio					X		X			X			X	
Oklahoma				X		X		X	X			X		
Oregon				X		X			X		X			

STATE	KG	1	2	3	4	5	6	7	8	9	10	11	12	COMMENT
Pennsylvania						X	X		X	X		X		
Rhode Island				X	X	X		X	X	X	X			
South Carolina				X	X	X	X	X	X	X	X			
South Dakota			X		X	X			X	X		X		
Tennessee			X	X	X	X	X	X	X			X		
Texas				X	X	X	X	X	X		X			
Utah		X	X	X	X	X	X	X	X	X	X	X	X	
Vermont					X	X	X		X	X	X	X		Rated by FairTest.Org as a nearly model system for assessment.
Virginia				X	X	X	X		X	X		X		
Washington					X			X			X			
West Virginia		X	X	X	X	X	X	X	X	X	X	X		
Wisconsin					X				X		X			
Wyoming					X				X			X		

Testing Accommodations

The more testing procedures vary from one classroom or school to the next, the less we can compare the scores from one group to another. Consider a test in which the publisher recommends that three sections of the test be given in one 45-minute session per day on three consecutive days. School A follows those directions. To save time, School B gives all three sections of the test in one session lasting slightly more than two hours. We can't say that both schools followed the same testing procedures. Remember that the test publishers provide testing procedures so schools can administer the tests in as close a manner as possible to the way the tests were administered to the groups used to obtain test norms. When we compare students' scores to norms, we want to compare apples to apples, not apples to oranges.

Most schools justifiably resist making any changes in testing procedures. Informally, a teacher can make minor changes that don't alter the testing procedures, such as separating two students who talk with each other instead of paying attention to the test; letting Lisa, who is getting over an ear infection, sit closer to the front so she can hear better; or moving Jeffrey away from the window to prevent his looking out the window and daydreaming.

There are two groups of students who require more formal testing accommodations. One group of students is identified as having a disability under Section 504 of the Rehabilitation Act of 1973 (Public Law 93-112). These students face some challenge but, with reasonable and appropriate accommodation, can take advantage of the same educational opportunities as other students. That is, they have a condition that requires some accommodation for them.

Just as schools must remove physical barriers to accommodate students with disabilities, they must make appropriate accommodations to remove other types of barriers to students' access to education. Marie is profoundly deaf, even with strong hearing aids. She does well in school with the aid of an interpreter, who signs her teacher's instructions to her and tells her teacher what Marie says in reply. An appropriate accommodation for Marie would be to provide the interpreter to sign test instructions to her, or to allow her to watch a videotape with an interpreter signing test instructions. Such a reasonable accommodation would not deviate from standard testing procedures and, in fact, would ensure that Marie received the same instructions as the other students.

If your child is considered disabled and has what is generally called a Section 504 Plan or individual accommodation plan (IAP), then the appropriate way to ask for testing accommodations is to ask for them in a meeting to discuss school accommodations under the plan. If your child is not already covered by such a plan, he or she won't qualify for one merely because you request testing accommodations.

The other group of students who may receive formal testing accommodations are those identified as handicapped under the Individuals with Disabilities Education Act (IDEA)—students with mental retardation, learning disabilities, serious emotional disturbance, orthopedic handicap, hearing or visual problems, and other handicaps defined in the law. These students have been identified under procedures governed by federal and sometimes state law, and their education is governed by a document called the Individualized Educational Program (IEP). Unless you are under a court order specifically revoking your educational rights on behalf of your child, you are a full member of the IEP team even if you and your child's other parent are divorced and the other parent has custody. Until recently, IEP teams actually had the prerogative to exclude certain handicapped students from taking standardized group testing altogether. However, today states make it more difficult to exclude students from testing.

If your child is classified as handicapped and has an IEP, the appropriate place to ask for testing accommodations is in an IEP team meeting. In fact, federal regulations require IEP teams to address testing accommodations. You have the right to call a meeting at any time. In that meeting, you will have the opportunity to present your case for the accommodations you believe are necessary. Be prepared for the other team members to resist making extreme accommodations unless you can present a very strong case. If your child is identified as handicapped and you believe that he or she should be provided special testing accommodations, contact the person at your child's school who is responsible for convening IEP meetings and request a meeting to discuss testing accommodations.

Problems arise when a request is made for accommodations that cause major departures from standard testing procedures. For example, Lynn has an identified learning disability in mathematics calculation and attends resource classes for math. Her disability is so severe that her IEP calls for her to use a calculator when performing all math problems. She fully under-

stands math concepts, but she simply can't perform the calculations without the aid of a calculator. Now it's time for Lynn to take the school-based standardized tests, and she asks to use a calculator. In this case, since her IEP already requires her to be provided with a calculator when performing math calculations, she may be allowed a calculator during school standardized tests. However, because using a calculator constitutes a major violation of standard testing procedures, her score on all sections in which she is allowed to use a calculator will be recorded as a failure, and her results in some states will be removed from among those of other students in her school in calculating school results.

How do we determine whether a student is allowed formal accommodations in standardized school testing and what these accommodations may be? First, if your child is not already identified as either handicapped or disabled, having the child classified in either group solely to receive testing accommodations will be considered a violation of the laws governing both classifications. Second, even if your child is already classified in either group, your state's department of public instruction will provide strict guidelines for the testing accommodations schools may make. Third, even if your child is classified in either group and you are proposing testing accommodations allowed under state testing guidelines, any accommodations must still be both *reasonable* and *appropriate*. To be reasonable and appropriate, testing accommodations must relate to your child's disability and must be similar to those already in place in his or her daily educational program. If your child is always tested individually in a separate room for all tests in all subjects, then a similar practice in taking school-based standardized tests may be appropriate. But if your child has a learning disability only in mathematics calculation, requesting that all test questions be read to him or her is inappropriate because that accommodation does not relate to his identified handicap.

Glossary

Accountability The idea that a school district is held responsible for the achievement of its students. The term may also be applied to holding students responsible for a certain level of achievement in order to be promoted or to graduate.

Achievement test An assessment that measures current knowledge in one or more of the areas taught in most schools, such as reading, math, and language arts.

Aptitude test An assessment designed to predict a student's potential for learning knowledge or skills.

Content validity The extent to which a test represents the content it is designed to cover.

Criterion-referenced test A test that rates how thoroughly a student has mastered a specific skill or area of knowledge. Typically, a criterion-referenced test is subjective, and relies on someone to observe and rate student work; it doesn't allow for easy comparisons of achievement among students. Performance assessments are criterion-referenced tests. The opposite of a criterion-referenced test is a norm-referenced test.

Frequency distribution A tabulation of individual scores (or groups of scores) that shows the number of persons who obtained each score.

Generalizability The idea that the score on a test reflects what a child knows about a subject, or how well he performs the skills the test is supposed to be assessing. Generalizability requires that enough test items are administered to truly assess a student's achievement.

Grade equivalent A score on a scale developed to indicate the school grade (usually measured in months of a year) that corresponds to an average chronological age, mental age, test score, or other characteristic. A grade equivalent of 6.4 is interpreted as a score that is average for a group in the fourth month of Grade 6.

High-stakes assessment A type of standardized test that has major consequences for a student or school (such as whether a child graduates from high school or gets admitted to college).

Mean Average score of a group of scores.

Median The middle score in a set of scores ranked from smallest to largest.

National percentile Percentile score derived from the performance of a group of individuals across the nation.

Normative sample A comparison group consisting of individuals who have taken a test under standard conditions.

Norm-referenced test   A standardized test that can compare scores of students in one school with a reference group (usually other students in the same grade and age, called the "norm group"). Norm-referenced tests compare the achievement of one student or the students of a school, school district, or state with the norm score.

Norms   A summary of the performance of a group of individuals on which a test was standardized.

Percentile   An incorrect form of the word *centile,* which is the percent of a group of scores that falls below a given score. Although the correct term is *centile,* much of the testing literature has adopted the term *percentile.*

Performance standards   A level of performance on a test set by education experts.

Quartiles   Points that divide the frequency distribution of scores into equal fourths.

Regression to the mean   The tendency of scores in a group of scores to vary in the direction of the mean. For example: If a child has an abnormally low score on a test, she is likely to make a higher score (that is, one closer to the mean) the next time she takes the test.

Reliability   The consistency with which a test measures some trait or characteristic. A measure can be reliable without being valid, but it can't be valid without being reliable.

Standard deviation   A statistical measure used to describe the extent to which scores vary in a group of scores. Approximately 68 percent of scores in a group are expected to be in a range from one standard deviation below the mean to one standard deviation above the mean.

Standardized test   A test that contains well-defined questions of proven validity and that produces reliable scores. Such tests are commonly paper-and-pencil exams containing multiple-choice items, true or false questions, matching exercises, or short fill-in-the-blanks items. These tests may also include performance assessment items (such as a writing sample), but assessment items cannot be completed quickly or scored reliably.

Test anxiety   Anxiety that occurs in test-taking situations. Test anxiety can seriously impair individuals' ability to obtain accurate scores on a test.

Validity   The extent to which a test measures the trait or characteristic it is designed to measure. Also see *reliability.*

Answer Keys for Practice Skills

Chapter 2: Word Analysis

1	D
2	C
3	B
4	A
5	D
6	D
7	B
8	B
9	A
10	C
11	C
12	A
13	B
14	A
15	D
16	A
17	C
18	B
19	C

Chapter 3: Vocabulary

1	A
2	C
3	D
4	D
5	D
6	D
7	A
8	B
9	C

10	C
11	B
12	D
13	D
14	B
15	A
16	C
17	A
18	D
19	B
20	C
21	A
22	C
23	C
24	A
25	C
26	B
27	C

Chapter 4: Reading Comprehension

1	D
2	B
3	C
4	B
5	A
6	A
7	B
8	C
9	A
10	B
11	C

12	D
13	A
14	B
15	B

Chapter 5: Listening

1	A
2	D
3	D
4	B
5	B
6	C
7	A

Chapter 6: Language Mechanics

1	C
2	A
3	B
4	B
5	C
6	C
7	C
8	A
9	B
10	B
11	B
12	D
13	B
14	D

15	B
16	D
17	D

Chapter 7: Spelling

1	A
2	D
3	C
4	C
5	C
6	D
7	C
8	C

Chapter 8: Math Concepts

1	D
2	B
3	B
4	B
5	C
6	C
7	C
8	A
9	C
10	D
11	A
12	B
13	C
14	A
15	B

16	C	5	D	3	D	12	C
17	C	6	A	4	A	13	A
		7	B	5	D	14	B
		8	B	6	B	15	D

Chapter 9:
Math Computation

1	C
2	B
3	B
4	A

7	B
8	B
9	C
10	D
11	A

Chapter 10:
Math Applications

1	B
2	C

Sample Practice Test

This following sample test provides 225 questions organized by the skill areas presented in the preceding chapters. The sample test is intended to provide a rough idea of the types of test questions your child will probably encounter on the commercial standardized tests provided at school. It is not an exact copy.

How to Use the Test

Although it's tempting to provide guidelines to try to mimic actual testing conditions children will face in school, we chose not to do so. First, many first graders find the standardized testing procedures in school to be grueling, and we didn't wish to subject your child to a simulation that might actually increase his anxiety toward school-based standardized tests.

Second, school-based standardized tests are timed, and many children simply don't work quickly enough to finish major sections of the tests. So your child's scores on school-based standardized tests reflect both the child's mastery of the subject areas and her ability to work quickly in a timed setting. In this guide, we are more concerned with strengthening certain skills than with the ability to work under time constraints.

We don't recommend that you attempt to simulate actual testing conditions. We suggest the following alternatives for using this test:

1. Administer the test to your child after you have completed all skills chapters and have begun to implement the strategies we suggested. Allow your child to work at a leisurely pace, probably 20- to 30-minute sessions spread out over several days.

2. Administer the pertinent section of the test after you have been through each chapter and implemented the strategies.

3. Use the test as a pretest rather than as a posttest, to identify the skills on which your child needs the most work. Then concentrate most of your efforts on the skills on which your child scores the lowest.

4. Administer each section of the test before you go through each chapter as a kind of skills check to help you determine how much of your energy you need to devote to that skill area.

Administering the Test

You will need to cut out the Sample Practice Test, including the Parent Script for the Listening test. Allow your child to write in the margins as needed, such as for figuring out math problems.

Don't provide any help to your child during these tests, but note specific problems. For example, if your child has problems reading math sentences, note whether the problem is with reading rather than with math. If your child's answer sheet looks sloppy, with many erasures or cross-outs, note that you need to work on neatness. (Remember that answer sheets on tests administered at school will be machine-scored, and the scanners sometimes mistake sloppily erased answers as the answers the child intends.)

Remember to be gentle with your child during testing. If your child needs to go to the toilet or get up and get a drink, that's fine. In this test, we are more interested in gauging your child's ability in each skill area than in his ability to adhere to inflexible testing conditions.

Scoring the Test

Use the Answer Key to score your child's answers. Then enter the scores in the table below.

TEST	NUMBER CORRECT	PERCENT CORRECT	LEVEL
WORD ANALYSIS			
VOCABULARY			
READING COMPREHENSION			
LISTENING			
LANGUAGE MECHANICS			
SPELLING			
MATH CONCEPTS			
MATH COMPUTATION			
MATH APPLICATIONS			

For your convenience, here is a table to convert the number correct in each 25-question section to the percent correct:

NUMBER CORRECT	PERCENT CORRECT	NUMBER CORRECT	PERCENT CORRECT
1	4	14	56
2	8	15	60
3	12	16	64
4	16	17	68
5	20	18	72
6	24	19	76
7	28	20	80
8	32	21	84
9	36	22	88
10	40	23	92
11	44	24	96
12	48	25	100
13	52		

Interpreting the Results

As you read the following interpretations of your child's scores, remember that they are only very rough, general interpretation guidelines.

% CORRECT	INTERPRETATION
0-59	DEFINITELY NEEDS WORK
60-79	NEEDS SOME WORK
80-89	GOOD
90-100	EXCELLENT

To the Student:

These tests will give you a chance to put the tips you have learned to work. A few last reminders . . .

- Be sure you understand all the directions before you begin each test. You may ask the teacher questions about the directions if you do not understand them.

- Work as quickly as you can during each test.

- When you change an answer, be sure to erase your first mark completely.

- You can guess at an answer or skip difficult items and go back to them later.

- Use the tips you have learned whenever you can.

- It is OK to be a little nervous. You may even do better.

Now that you have completed the lessons in this book, you are on your way to scoring high!

STUDENT'S NAME																		SCHOOL

LAST · FIRST · MI

TEACHER

FEMALE ◯   MALE ◯

BIRTHDATE

MONTH	DAY	YEAR
JAN ◯	⓪ ⓪	⓪
FEB ◯	① ①	①
MAR ◯	② ②	②
APR ◯	③ ③	③
MAY ◯	④	④
JUN ◯	⑤	⑤ ⑤
JUL ◯	⑥	⑥ ⑥
AUG ◯	⑦	⑦ ⑦
SEP ◯	⑧	⑧ ⑧
OCT ◯	⑨	⑨ ⑨
NOV ◯		
DEC ◯		

GRADE

① ② ③ ④ ⑤ ⑥

(Name grid columns A–Z with bubbles for each letter)

Grade 1 Name and Answer Sheet

Word Analysis

1 Ⓐ Ⓑ Ⓒ Ⓓ	6 Ⓐ Ⓑ Ⓒ Ⓓ	10 Ⓐ Ⓑ Ⓒ Ⓓ	14 Ⓐ Ⓑ Ⓒ Ⓓ	18 Ⓐ Ⓑ Ⓒ Ⓓ	22 Ⓐ Ⓑ Ⓒ Ⓓ
2 Ⓐ Ⓑ Ⓒ Ⓓ	7 Ⓐ Ⓑ Ⓒ Ⓓ	11 Ⓐ Ⓑ Ⓒ Ⓓ	15 Ⓐ Ⓑ Ⓒ Ⓓ	19 Ⓐ Ⓑ Ⓒ Ⓓ	23 Ⓐ Ⓑ Ⓒ Ⓓ
3 Ⓐ Ⓑ Ⓒ Ⓓ	8 Ⓐ Ⓑ Ⓒ Ⓓ	12 Ⓐ Ⓑ Ⓒ Ⓓ	16 Ⓐ Ⓑ Ⓒ Ⓓ	20 Ⓐ Ⓑ Ⓒ Ⓓ	24 Ⓐ Ⓑ Ⓒ Ⓓ
4 Ⓐ Ⓑ Ⓒ Ⓓ	9 Ⓐ Ⓑ Ⓒ Ⓓ	13 Ⓐ Ⓑ Ⓒ Ⓓ	17 Ⓐ Ⓑ Ⓒ Ⓓ	21 Ⓐ Ⓑ Ⓒ Ⓓ	25 Ⓐ Ⓑ Ⓒ Ⓓ
5 Ⓐ Ⓑ Ⓒ Ⓓ					

Vocabulary

1 Ⓐ Ⓑ Ⓒ Ⓓ	6 Ⓐ Ⓑ Ⓒ Ⓓ	10 Ⓐ Ⓑ Ⓒ Ⓓ	14 Ⓐ Ⓑ Ⓒ Ⓓ	18 Ⓐ Ⓑ Ⓒ Ⓓ	22 Ⓐ Ⓑ Ⓒ Ⓓ
2 Ⓐ Ⓑ Ⓒ Ⓓ	7 Ⓐ Ⓑ Ⓒ Ⓓ	11 Ⓐ Ⓑ Ⓒ Ⓓ	15 Ⓐ Ⓑ Ⓒ Ⓓ	19 Ⓐ Ⓑ Ⓒ Ⓓ	23 Ⓐ Ⓑ Ⓒ Ⓓ
3 Ⓐ Ⓑ Ⓒ Ⓓ	8 Ⓐ Ⓑ Ⓒ Ⓓ	12 Ⓐ Ⓑ Ⓒ Ⓓ	16 Ⓐ Ⓑ Ⓒ Ⓓ	20 Ⓐ Ⓑ Ⓒ Ⓓ	24 Ⓐ Ⓑ Ⓒ Ⓓ
4 Ⓐ Ⓑ Ⓒ Ⓓ	9 Ⓐ Ⓑ Ⓒ Ⓓ	13 Ⓐ Ⓑ Ⓒ Ⓓ	17 Ⓐ Ⓑ Ⓒ Ⓓ	21 Ⓐ Ⓑ Ⓒ Ⓓ	25 Ⓐ Ⓑ Ⓒ Ⓓ
5 Ⓐ Ⓑ Ⓒ Ⓓ					

Reading Comprehension

1 Ⓐ Ⓑ Ⓒ Ⓓ	6 Ⓐ Ⓑ Ⓒ Ⓓ	10 Ⓐ Ⓑ Ⓒ Ⓓ	14 Ⓐ Ⓑ Ⓒ Ⓓ	18 Ⓐ Ⓑ Ⓒ Ⓓ	22 Ⓐ Ⓑ Ⓒ Ⓓ
2 Ⓐ Ⓑ Ⓒ Ⓓ	7 Ⓐ Ⓑ Ⓒ Ⓓ	11 Ⓐ Ⓑ Ⓒ Ⓓ	15 Ⓐ Ⓑ Ⓒ Ⓓ	19 Ⓐ Ⓑ Ⓒ Ⓓ	23 Ⓐ Ⓑ Ⓒ Ⓓ
3 Ⓐ Ⓑ Ⓒ Ⓓ	8 Ⓐ Ⓑ Ⓒ Ⓓ	12 Ⓐ Ⓑ Ⓒ Ⓓ	16 Ⓐ Ⓑ Ⓒ Ⓓ	20 Ⓐ Ⓑ Ⓒ Ⓓ	24 Ⓐ Ⓑ Ⓒ Ⓓ
4 Ⓐ Ⓑ Ⓒ Ⓓ	9 Ⓐ Ⓑ Ⓒ Ⓓ	13 Ⓐ Ⓑ Ⓒ Ⓓ	17 Ⓐ Ⓑ Ⓒ Ⓓ	21 Ⓐ Ⓑ Ⓒ Ⓓ	25 Ⓐ Ⓑ Ⓒ Ⓓ
5 Ⓐ Ⓑ Ⓒ Ⓓ					

Listening

1 Ⓐ Ⓑ Ⓒ Ⓓ	6 Ⓐ Ⓑ Ⓒ Ⓓ	10 Ⓐ Ⓑ Ⓒ Ⓓ	14 Ⓐ Ⓑ Ⓒ Ⓓ	18 Ⓐ Ⓑ Ⓒ Ⓓ	22 Ⓐ Ⓑ Ⓒ Ⓓ
2 Ⓐ Ⓑ Ⓒ Ⓓ	7 Ⓐ Ⓑ Ⓒ Ⓓ	11 Ⓐ Ⓑ Ⓒ Ⓓ	15 Ⓐ Ⓑ Ⓒ Ⓓ	19 Ⓐ Ⓑ Ⓒ Ⓓ	23 Ⓐ Ⓑ Ⓒ Ⓓ
3 Ⓐ Ⓑ Ⓒ Ⓓ	8 Ⓐ Ⓑ Ⓒ Ⓓ	12 Ⓐ Ⓑ Ⓒ Ⓓ	16 Ⓐ Ⓑ Ⓒ Ⓓ	20 Ⓐ Ⓑ Ⓒ Ⓓ	24 Ⓐ Ⓑ Ⓒ Ⓓ
4 Ⓐ Ⓑ Ⓒ Ⓓ	9 Ⓐ Ⓑ Ⓒ Ⓓ	13 Ⓐ Ⓑ Ⓒ Ⓓ	17 Ⓐ Ⓑ Ⓒ Ⓓ	21 Ⓐ Ⓑ Ⓒ Ⓓ	25 Ⓐ Ⓑ Ⓒ Ⓓ
5 Ⓐ Ⓑ Ⓒ Ⓓ					

Language Mechanics

1 Ⓐ Ⓑ Ⓒ Ⓓ	6 Ⓐ Ⓑ Ⓒ Ⓓ	10 Ⓐ Ⓑ Ⓒ Ⓓ	14 Ⓐ Ⓑ Ⓒ Ⓓ	18 Ⓐ Ⓑ Ⓒ Ⓓ	22 Ⓐ Ⓑ Ⓒ Ⓓ
2 Ⓐ Ⓑ Ⓒ Ⓓ	7 Ⓐ Ⓑ Ⓒ Ⓓ	11 Ⓐ Ⓑ Ⓒ Ⓓ	15 Ⓐ Ⓑ Ⓒ Ⓓ	19 Ⓐ Ⓑ Ⓒ Ⓓ	23 Ⓐ Ⓑ Ⓒ Ⓓ
3 Ⓐ Ⓑ Ⓒ Ⓓ	8 Ⓐ Ⓑ Ⓒ Ⓓ	12 Ⓐ Ⓑ Ⓒ Ⓓ	16 Ⓐ Ⓑ Ⓒ Ⓓ	20 Ⓐ Ⓑ Ⓒ Ⓓ	24 Ⓐ Ⓑ Ⓒ Ⓓ
4 Ⓐ Ⓑ Ⓒ Ⓓ	9 Ⓐ Ⓑ Ⓒ Ⓓ	13 Ⓐ Ⓑ Ⓒ Ⓓ	17 Ⓐ Ⓑ Ⓒ Ⓓ	21 Ⓐ Ⓑ Ⓒ Ⓓ	25 Ⓐ Ⓑ Ⓒ Ⓓ
5 Ⓐ Ⓑ Ⓒ Ⓓ					

Spelling

1 Ⓐ Ⓑ Ⓒ Ⓓ	6 Ⓐ Ⓑ Ⓒ Ⓓ	10 Ⓐ Ⓑ Ⓒ Ⓓ	14 Ⓐ Ⓑ Ⓒ Ⓓ	18 Ⓐ Ⓑ Ⓒ Ⓓ	22 Ⓐ Ⓑ Ⓒ Ⓓ
2 Ⓐ Ⓑ Ⓒ Ⓓ	7 Ⓐ Ⓑ Ⓒ Ⓓ	11 Ⓐ Ⓑ Ⓒ Ⓓ	15 Ⓐ Ⓑ Ⓒ Ⓓ	19 Ⓐ Ⓑ Ⓒ Ⓓ	23 Ⓐ Ⓑ Ⓒ Ⓓ
3 Ⓐ Ⓑ Ⓒ Ⓓ	8 Ⓐ Ⓑ Ⓒ Ⓓ	12 Ⓐ Ⓑ Ⓒ Ⓓ	16 Ⓐ Ⓑ Ⓒ Ⓓ	20 Ⓐ Ⓑ Ⓒ Ⓓ	24 Ⓐ Ⓑ Ⓒ Ⓓ
4 Ⓐ Ⓑ Ⓒ Ⓓ	9 Ⓐ Ⓑ Ⓒ Ⓓ	13 Ⓐ Ⓑ Ⓒ Ⓓ	17 Ⓐ Ⓑ Ⓒ Ⓓ	21 Ⓐ Ⓑ Ⓒ Ⓓ	25 Ⓐ Ⓑ Ⓒ Ⓓ
5 Ⓐ Ⓑ Ⓒ Ⓓ					

Math Concepts

1 Ⓐ Ⓑ Ⓒ Ⓓ	6 Ⓐ Ⓑ Ⓒ Ⓓ	10 Ⓐ Ⓑ Ⓒ Ⓓ	14 Ⓐ Ⓑ Ⓒ Ⓓ	18 Ⓐ Ⓑ Ⓒ Ⓓ	22 Ⓐ Ⓑ Ⓒ Ⓓ
2 Ⓐ Ⓑ Ⓒ Ⓓ	7 Ⓐ Ⓑ Ⓒ Ⓓ	11 Ⓐ Ⓑ Ⓒ Ⓓ	15 Ⓐ Ⓑ Ⓒ Ⓓ	19 Ⓐ Ⓑ Ⓒ Ⓓ	23 Ⓐ Ⓑ Ⓒ Ⓓ
3 Ⓐ Ⓑ Ⓒ Ⓓ	8 Ⓐ Ⓑ Ⓒ Ⓓ	12 Ⓐ Ⓑ Ⓒ Ⓓ	16 Ⓐ Ⓑ Ⓒ Ⓓ	20 Ⓐ Ⓑ Ⓒ Ⓓ	24 Ⓐ Ⓑ Ⓒ Ⓓ
4 Ⓐ Ⓑ Ⓒ Ⓓ	9 Ⓐ Ⓑ Ⓒ Ⓓ	13 Ⓐ Ⓑ Ⓒ Ⓓ	17 Ⓐ Ⓑ Ⓒ Ⓓ	21 Ⓐ Ⓑ Ⓒ Ⓓ	25 Ⓐ Ⓑ Ⓒ Ⓓ
5 Ⓐ Ⓑ Ⓒ Ⓓ					

Math Computation

1 Ⓐ Ⓑ Ⓒ Ⓓ	6 Ⓐ Ⓑ Ⓒ Ⓓ	10 Ⓐ Ⓑ Ⓒ Ⓓ	14 Ⓐ Ⓑ Ⓒ Ⓓ	18 Ⓐ Ⓑ Ⓒ Ⓓ	22 Ⓐ Ⓑ Ⓒ Ⓓ
2 Ⓐ Ⓑ Ⓒ Ⓓ	7 Ⓐ Ⓑ Ⓒ Ⓓ	11 Ⓐ Ⓑ Ⓒ Ⓓ	15 Ⓐ Ⓑ Ⓒ Ⓓ	19 Ⓐ Ⓑ Ⓒ Ⓓ	23 Ⓐ Ⓑ Ⓒ Ⓓ
3 Ⓐ Ⓑ Ⓒ Ⓓ	8 Ⓐ Ⓑ Ⓒ Ⓓ	12 Ⓐ Ⓑ Ⓒ Ⓓ	16 Ⓐ Ⓑ Ⓒ Ⓓ	20 Ⓐ Ⓑ Ⓒ Ⓓ	24 Ⓐ Ⓑ Ⓒ Ⓓ
4 Ⓐ Ⓑ Ⓒ Ⓓ	9 Ⓐ Ⓑ Ⓒ Ⓓ	13 Ⓐ Ⓑ Ⓒ Ⓓ	17 Ⓐ Ⓑ Ⓒ Ⓓ	21 Ⓐ Ⓑ Ⓒ Ⓓ	25 Ⓐ Ⓑ Ⓒ Ⓓ
5 Ⓐ Ⓑ Ⓒ Ⓓ					

Math Applications

1 Ⓐ Ⓑ Ⓒ Ⓓ	6 Ⓐ Ⓑ Ⓒ Ⓓ	10 Ⓐ Ⓑ Ⓒ Ⓓ	14 Ⓐ Ⓑ Ⓒ Ⓓ	18 Ⓐ Ⓑ Ⓒ Ⓓ	22 Ⓐ Ⓑ Ⓒ Ⓓ
2 Ⓐ Ⓑ Ⓒ Ⓓ	7 Ⓐ Ⓑ Ⓒ Ⓓ	11 Ⓐ Ⓑ Ⓒ Ⓓ	15 Ⓐ Ⓑ Ⓒ Ⓓ	19 Ⓐ Ⓑ Ⓒ Ⓓ	23 Ⓐ Ⓑ Ⓒ Ⓓ
3 Ⓐ Ⓑ Ⓒ Ⓓ	8 Ⓐ Ⓑ Ⓒ Ⓓ	12 Ⓐ Ⓑ Ⓒ Ⓓ	16 Ⓐ Ⓑ Ⓒ Ⓓ	20 Ⓐ Ⓑ Ⓒ Ⓓ	24 Ⓐ Ⓑ Ⓒ Ⓓ
4 Ⓐ Ⓑ Ⓒ Ⓓ	9 Ⓐ Ⓑ Ⓒ Ⓓ	13 Ⓐ Ⓑ Ⓒ Ⓓ	17 Ⓐ Ⓑ Ⓒ Ⓓ	21 Ⓐ Ⓑ Ⓒ Ⓓ	25 Ⓐ Ⓑ Ⓒ Ⓓ
5 Ⓐ Ⓑ Ⓒ Ⓓ					

WORD ANALYSIS

Directions: Read each question and choose the correct answer.

Example:

An animal that says "meow" is a __at.

A b

B h

C c

D r

Answer:

C An animal that says "meow" is a <u>c</u>at.

1 Here is a picture of a __og. What is the first letter?

A f

B p

C d

D g

2 What letter goes in the blank? L M N O __ Q R

A R

B P

C S

D T

3 Which of these pairs of letters show <u>different</u> letters?

A F   f

B T   t

C Q   q

D B   d

4 <u>A</u> is for <u>apple</u>, <u>B</u> is for <u>boy</u>. <u>G</u> is for <u>what</u>?

A bicycle   **B** duck

C fish   **D** girl

5 Choose the word that has the same <u>beginning</u> sound as in <u>television</u>.

A danger   **B** turtle

C football   **D** basket

6 Choose the word that has the same <u>ending</u> sound as in <u>plant</u>.

A ant

B place

C purple

D rip

7 Choose the name of a flower that rhymes with <u>nose</u>.

A neck

B rose

C note

D zoo

8 Find the missing word in this sentence: It was time for my soccer game, so Dad said he would ___ me to the park.

A taken

B took

C bring

D take

9 <u>Under</u> means the same thing as what?

A not over   **B** in front of

C behind   **D** instead of

10 Choose the one that means the most of something.

A loudest

B loud

C louder

D loudent

11 Which two words rhyme?

A saw, was

B boo, boy

C bear, fair

D then, them

12 Which word is made up of two different words?

A flooded

B football

C undone

D maker

13 Don't means the same thing as:

A cannot

B do now

C do it

D do not

GO

14 Here is a picture of a __ire. What letter goes in the blank?

A q   **B** t

C p   **D** f

---

15 Here is a part of the alphabet: U V W ___ Y Z. Which letter is missing?

A w   **B** x

C y   **D** z

Directions for Questions 16–20: Say the word for each question. Look at the underlined part of the word. Then find the word that has the same sound as the underlined part.

Example: b<u>oo</u>t

A bear   **B** hoot

C bait   **D** bit

Answer:

B hoot

16 r<u>o</u>ll

    A smoke

    B ran

    C roof

    D call

---

17 b<u>ea</u>r

    A bone

    B fear

    C boat

    D napkin

---

18 h<u>oo</u>t

    A help

    B shoot

    C tone

    D owl

---

19 forg<u>e</u>t

    A forge

    B goof

    C wed

    D taken

GO ⇨

20 c<u>a</u>r

    A cat   **B** care

    C hog   **D** make

Directions for Questions 21–25:
Fill in the blanks in these questions.

Example:

The table is made of ___ood.

    A h   **B** w

    C f   **D** g

Answer:

    B w   The table is made of wood.

---

21 The window is made of __lass.

    A k   **B** g

    C c   **D** q

---

22 I will ride my bike tomorrow. Yesterday I _____ my bike.

    A rid   **B** road

    C rode   **D** ride

---

23 First one leaf fell off of the tree. Then two more ___ fell.

    A leafs   **B** leaves

    C levers   **D** left

---

24 Finish this poem with something that rhymes: In spring or winter or summer or fall, when Grandma comes, we have a ___.

    A ball

    B party

    C cookie

    D good time

25 This is a picture of a tr__

    A ee   **B** oo

    C e   **D** i

STOP

VOCABULARY

Directions: Read the following questions and choose the correct answers.

Example:

A baby dog is a _____.

A piglet   **B** cygnet

C kitten   **D** puppy

Answer:

D puppy   A baby dog is a puppy.

1 Choose the picture that shows <u>repairing</u>.

A   **B**

C

D

2 How is the man in this picture feeling?

A unhappy   **B** happy

C surprised   **D** angry

3 Choose the word that means "baby cat."

A kitten   **B** catty

C lamb   **D** joey

4 What do we call a group of people on the same side in a game?

A tribe   **B** gang

C family   **D** team

5 Choose the word that means "to give something back to its owner."

A steal   **B** borrow

C lend   **D** return

6 Choose the sentence that goes with the word <u>tie</u>.

  A Big sister has one in her pocketbook in case she gets hurt.

  B Men put this around their necks and make a knot.

  C This goes around a bicycle wheel.

  D We put grocery bags in this.

7 Fill in the blank: Karen dropped her purse and spilled her money, keys, and ___ onto the floor.

  A belt   **B** eye

  C shoe   **D** comb

8 Choose the pair of words that mean the same.

  A late, tardy

  B fat, thin

  C old, date

  D green, blue

9 Choose the pair of words that mean the opposite.

  A left, right

  B around, behind

  C behind, below

  D around, under

10 Choose the word that means the same as the underlined word in this sentence: When the <u>car</u> stopped, Jeffrey got out.

  A automobile   **B** tram

  C cart   **D** trailer

11 Choose the word that means the opposite of the underlined word in this sentence: I liked the cake, but it was <u>dry</u>.

  A chocolate   **B** hot

  C cold   **D** wet

12 Fill in the blank: Billy's mother said, "Billy, could you help me? I spilled a glass of milk. Could you go get me the ___?"

  A broom   **B** mop

  C glass   **D** juice

13 Choose the best word to finish this sentence: The first cookie was not too bad. The second cookie was worse. But the third cookie was the ___.

  A worst

  B worsest

  C worse

  D worser

GO

Directions for Questions 14, 15, and 16: Choose the word in each group that goes with the picture below.

14 A cow   **B** goat

     C chicken   **D** mule

15 A corn   **B** hay

     C beans   **D** bricks

16 A shovels   **B** lamps

     C hoes   **D** wheels

17 Choose the sentence that is true about the picture.

     A The seal is over the ball.

     B The ball is behind the seal.

     C The ball is under the seal.

     D The seal is under the ball.

18 Choose the sentence that is true about the picture.

     A The worm is inside the apple.

     B The apple is inside the worm.

     C The worm is beside the apple.

     D The apple is beside the worm.

Directions for Questions 19–25: Choose the word that goes with each definition.

Example: What you wear on your head.

     A clown

     B hat

     C shoes

     D cat

Answer:

     B hat

19 Make a hole with a shovel.

     A hoe

     B shovel

     C dig

     D hole

20 What you put your feet on to make your bicycle go.

A pedals

B handlebars

C chain

D wheel

21 What you do to your hands when they get dirty.

A water

B wash

C soap

D clean

22 infant

A baby

B picture

C diaper

D crawl

23 We cook on it.

A over

B staff

C cook

D stove

24 What we do to wood to keep it from rotting in the rain.

A burn

B paint

C cut

D saw

25 What we put on furniture to make it pretty.

A water

B polish

C bricks

D nails

STOP

READING COMPREHENSION

Directions for Questions 1–10:
Parents: Read the stories to your child, then ask the questions and read the possible answers. Say this: "Listen to what I say. I will ask you questions about it."

Story: Michael lived way out in the country. He and his friend Robert enjoyed making boats out of paper and sailing them down Caney Creek. They pretended that the boats were pirate ships and pretended that the pirates on the ships fought for treasure. One day, a cricket jumped in one of the boats and rode the boat until it was out of sight. "Look," Michael said, "the cricket stole my boat."

1 Where did Michael live?

A in the country

B on a mountain

C in town

D out near the ball field

2 What was Michael's friend's name?

A Thomas

B Linda

C Robert

D Carol

3 What did Michael and his friend build?

A pirate forts

B airplanes

C kites

D boats

4 What did they pretend?

A that they were explorers looking for lost cities

B that they were lion hunters in Africa

C that pirates fought each other for treasure

D that they were movie stars

5 What did Michael accuse the cricket of doing?

A eating his lunch

B biting him on the foot

C stealing his boat

D eating a hole in his shirt

Story: Grandmother looked around and asked, "Where is Paula?" Jenny did not see her little sister anywhere. She and Grandmother looked all over the house, but Paula was nowhere to be found. Just then, they heard a small child crying. Grandmother ran to the window and started to laugh. Paula had crawled through the door and out into the yard. She was just about to walk out into the street when Baxter saw her. Baxter had the seat of Paula's pants in his teeth and was dragging her back into the yard where she would be safe.

6 Who was Paula?

A Jenny's grandmother

B Jenny's little sister

C Grandmother's dog

D Baxter's grandmother

7 Where had Paula gone?

A She had gone out into the yard and was about to walk out into the street.

B She had gone into her bedroom and was asleep on the bed.

C She had gone into the bathroom and was running water for a bath.

D She had gone to work.

8 Why was Grandmother laughing?

A Jenny told her a joke.

B Paula said something funny.

C Baxter drew a funny picture.

D It was funny seeing Baxter drag Paula by the seat of her pants.

9 Why was Paula crying?

A Jenny had hit her.

B Grandmother would not allow her to play in the street.

C Grandmother was making her play outside.

D Baxter was dragging her by the seat of her pants.

10 Who do you think Baxter is?

A Jenny and Paula's grandfather

B Jenny and Paula's brother

C Grandmother's neighbor

D a dog

[*Note*: Your child continues from this point.]

Directions for Questions 11–20: Read these stories and then answer the questions.

GO

Example: I have fins and a tail. I swim in the water. I don't breathe air. What am I?

  A dog   **B** cat

  C fish   **D** clam

Answer:

  C fish

---

11 I am brown and green. I have a big shell on my back. If I am afraid, I pull my head and my legs into my shell. What am I?

  A a kangaroo **B** a mouse

  C a bat   **D** a turtle

Story for Questions 12 and 13: I sleep upside down all day in a cave. After the sun goes down, I fly around and eat lots of insects.

12 What am I?

  A an insect

  B a bird

  C an airplane

  D a bat

---

13 When do I fly around?

  A at night

  B on the weekend

  C during the day

  D only on Saturday

Story for Questions 14 to 16: T. J. could not find his skates. He first looked in his closet. Then he looked in the backyard. He saw something under the kitchen table and went to see what it was. He crawled under the table and came out with a big smile on his face.

14 What had T. J. lost?

  A his skates

  B his birthday money

  C his baby brother

  D his pencil

---

15 Where is the first place T. J. looked?

  A under the kitchen table

  B in the backyard

  C under the steps

  D in his closet

---

16 Why do you think T. J. was smiling when he came out from under the kitchen table?

  A He liked crawling under tables.

  B He found what he had lost.

  C He hit his head very hard.

  D He found his baby brother.

17 The golf ball was only six feet from the hole. Kristin hit the ball very carefully toward the hole. Then she looked angry and said, "Oh, no." What probably happened?

   A The ball did not go into the hole.

   B The ball went into the hole.

   C She lost her ball.

   D She found a ball someone else had lost.

Story for Questions 18 to 20: It was time for dinner, and Grandfather couldn't find Jamie anywhere. He had cooked hot dogs, Jamie's favorite food. He decided to go ahead and eat and went back into the kitchen. There sat Jamie at the kitchen table with her mouth full.

18 Who was Grandfather looking for?

   A Paula

   B Jamie's dog

   C Grandmother

   D Jamie

19 What did Grandfather decide to do when he could not find Jamie?

   A to go into the backyard to look for Jamie

   B to go back to the kitchen and eat

   C to go eat Jamie's hot dogs

   D to go watch television

20 What do you think Jamie had in her mouth?

   A hot dog   **B** candy

   C ice cream   **D** nothing

Directions for Questions 21 to 25: Choose the sentence that best tells about the picture.

21

   A The pirate had a wooden leg.

   B The pirate was afraid of what was in the bag.

   C The pirate did not know what he had found.

   D The pirate found treasure.

22

A   Mr. Allen has a grandson named Jake.

B   Mr. Allen bought a new truck.

C   Mr. Allen carries groceries in his truck.

D   Mr. Allen is not going anywhere.

23

A   Marie has to do her homework on the computer.

B   Marie enjoys playing games on her computer.

C   Marie does not know how to use her computer.

D   Marie has a school holiday tomorrow.

24

A   Gina and Sam are going to play golf.

B   Gina and Sam found a new place to ride their bikes.

C   Gina is helping Sam look for his puppy.

D   Gina and Sam are helping their mother take out the trash.

25

A   Buffy the hamster hates peanuts.

B   Buffy the hamster gets a treat.

C   Buffy the hamster gets a bath.

D   Buffy the hamster gets out of her cage.

PARENT SCRIPT FOR LISTENING TEST

Directions: Read the questions and answers to your child.

Parent: "Listen to each story. Then choose the best answer to the questions I ask. I may read the story only one time."

1 Jason and his grandmother like to watch birds. One day, a tiny bird flew up into the tree across the street. Grandmother said, "Jason, I think that is a Carolina Wren." To make sure it was a Carolina Wren, Jason and his grandmother went to get what?

2 When Mother found Sara, she was standing next to the broken window holding her baseball. Sara had a sad look on her face. Why do you think Sarah might be sad?

3 Lisa and her twin sister Linda built a snowman. They first put a large snowball on bottom, then a middle-size snowball for the middle, and then a smaller snowball for the head. They found an old hunter's hat with ear flaps and put it on the snowman's head. They used a carrot for the nose and broken tree branches for hands. Choose the picture that matches the story.

4 Justin stopped running to tie his shoe. Choose the picture that best illustrates the sentence.

5 Carley was playing Bingo. When the announcer called out, "B2 . . . B2," Carley put the marker on the B2 on her card and jumped up, clapping her hands. She shouted something. What did she shout?

Story for Questions 6–8

Joy was sitting on a rock in the middle of the river with her grandfather. Her grandfather told her about growing up during the Depression with no money. He told her, "We were so poor that we had to catch fish so that we would have enough to eat. But we were so poor that we could not afford fishing rods or hooks." Joy asked, "If you could not afford fishing rods or hooks, how did you catch the fish?" Her grandfather said, "Like this," and slid off the rock into the river. He bent down and came up with something in his hands.

6 Who was sitting on the rock with Joy?

7 What were they talking about?

8 When the man with Joy bent down into the river and came up

with something in his hands, what do you think he had?

Story for Questions 9–11

Not very many people weave nets by hand anymore, but Ross and his father do. They made a hammock for Ross' mother, a net for Uncle Bill's basketball goal, and shopping bags for the family to take with them to the fresh market. When the tennis net at his school tore, Ross was able to repair it.

9 What can we say about how popular net weaving by hand is?

10 Find the thing that Ross and his father did **not** make.

11 How did Ross get to use net weaving to help his school?

12 Jared was playing a board game. He had to make the word *football* out of the letters. What letters did he have?

Story for Questions 13–15

Anna studies karate at the community center. She started out as a white belt, but three months after she began, she earned her orange belt. Next week, she is going to test for her orange belt with one stripe. She is nervous, because to earn her belt

she must be able to break a board with her hand.

13 What is Anna doing at the community center?

14 What was the first belt that Anna earned?

15 Why is Anna nervous about her next test?

Story for Questions 16–19

Sam does not like litter. He and the other members of his Cub Scout pack have adopted one mile of Oak Street and pick up any litter they see there. Once a month, they take a lot of trash bags and pick up trash that people throw out of their cars.

16 What does Sam not like?

17 What group does Sam belong to?

18 What word means the same as *litter*?

19 What street do Sam and his friends keep free of litter?

Story for Questions 20–23

Jim went to spend a week with his cousin Joe who lived in the mountains. Joe asked, "Do you want to go deer slapping?" Jim thought he was kidding, but Joe said, "Come on." He took Jim deep into the woods. Joe got down on his stomach and smelled some ruts on the side of the trail.

"This is a good place," he said. "We can wait right over there." He pointed to a place behind some rocks, and he and Jim went there and waited. About an hour later, a big deer walked down the path and looked around.

Joe whispered, "Go on three." He then raised his fingers: one finger; two fingers; then three fingers. Joe jumped up, ran up to the deer, and patted it. The deer jumped and ran away. Jim thought to himself, "Boy, they sure do strange things for fun here in the mountains."

20 Whom did Jim go visit?

21 Where did Joe live?

22 What did Joe want to take Jim to do?

23 What did Jim think about what Joe did?

24 The bicycle shop had a sale on white bicycle tires. Choose the picture that shows what was on sale at the bicycle shop.

25 Marissa said, "Jack's head is so big that he has to wear two hats." What is wrong or silly about what Marissa said?

STOP

L I S T E N I N G

Directions: *Parents*: Read story from listening script.

Say to your child: "Listen to each story. Then choose the best answer to the questions I ask. I may read the story only one time."

1 A  **B**  **C**  **D**

---

2 A. She broke the window.

B She wanted to play ball, but it was raining.

C It was time to go to school.

D She did not want to play ball because she could not catch well.

---

3 A **B** **C**  **D**

---

4 A  **B** **C**  **D**

---

5 A May I be excused? **B** Bingo!

C Lynn is cheating! **D** I have to go home!

6 **A** her grandfather

   B her Uncle Jim

   C her grandmother

   D her father

7 **A** how Grandfather asked Grandmother to marry him

   B Joy's new friend at school

   C how poor the family was during the Depression

   D Joy's father's new job

8 **A** a fishing rod   **B** a fish

   C Joy's shoes   **D** a rock

9 **A** It is more popular today than ever.

   B For some reason, only women weave nets.

   C Not very many people weave nets by hand anymore.

   D It is not very popular because you must be left-handed to weave nets.

10 **A** a hammock for Ross' mother

   B a plant holder for Grandmother

   C a net for Uncle Bill's basketball goal

   D shopping bags for the family

11 **A** He repaired the tennis net.

   B He repaired the basketball net.

   C He repaired the soccer net.

   D He made shopping bags for the teachers.

12 **A** OWN ORD

   B OOF ENT

   C FOOD TALL

   D FOO ALL

13 **A** She takes karate.

   B She takes ballet.

   C She plays basketball.

   D She helps deliver meals to sick people.

14 **A** yellow

   B orange

   C green

   D black

15 **A** She has to be able jump over two chairs.

   B She must make a perfect score.

   C She must break a board with her hand.

   D She does not want to put stripe on her belt.

GO ▷

16 A small children

B people who drive cars

C picking up trash

D litter

---

17 A Campfire Explorers

B Boy Scouts

C Girl Scouts

D Cub Scouts

---

18 A leaves   **B** cars

C dirt   **D** trash

---

19 A Clinton Avenue

B Kellogg Way

C Maple Drive

D Oak Street

---

20 A his grandparents

B his cousin

C a friend from school

D a new boy on his street

---

21 A down the street

B over in Springfield

C out in the country

D in the mountains

---

22 A get a snack

B pick some apples

C go fishing

D deer slapping

---

23 A He thought it was strange.

B He thought it was boring.

C He admired what Joe did.

D He wanted to do it.

---

24 A   **B**

C

D

---

25 A Jack's head really is not very big.

B Marissa's head is bigger than Jack's.

C Putting two hats together would not make them fit Jack's head.

D People who have big heads do not wear hats.

STOP

LANGUAGE MECHANICS

Directions for Questions 1 to 4:
Read these sentences and pick out the words that should be capitalized.

Example:

susie came to my house today.

A susie   **B** came

C house   **D** today

Answer:

A susie   Susie came to my house today.

---

1 ginger followed the other cats down the street.

A cats   **B** ginger

C street   **D** down

---

2 The fire trucks went down Oak street.

A street   **B** fire

C trucks   **D** down

---

3 I think that peaches is the prettiest cat.

A think   **B** peaches

C prettiest   **D** cat

---

4 Jim rode his schwinn bicycle down the street.

A street

B bicycle

C rode

D schwinn

Directions for Questions 5 to 8:
Choose the sentence that has correct punctuation.

Example:

A Sandy wanted to see Sammys' horse.

B Sandy wanted to see Sammies horse.

C Sandy wanted to see Sammy's horse.

D Sandy wanted to see Sammys horse.

Answer:

C Sandy wanted to see Sammy's horse.

---

5 A Kristin broke Carlas jar.

B Kristin broke Carlas' jar

C Kristin' broke Carlas jar.

D Kristin broke Carla's jar.

---

6 A The peach pie was good but the apple pie was better.

B The peach pie was good, but the apple pie was better.

C The peach pie was good, but, the apple pie was better.

D The peach pie was good but the apple pie was better?

---

7 A Jamie likes baseball but cannot stand basketball.

B Jamie likes baseball, but cannot stand basketball.

C Jamie likes baseball. But cannot stand basketball.

D Jamie likes baseball but, cannot stand basketball.

---

8 A Which ball belongs to Jean?

B Which ball belongs to Jean.

C Which ball belong's to Jean?

D Which ball belongs to Jean!

Directions for Questions 9 to 12:
Read each sentence and then choose the correct pronoun for the underlined word or words.

Example: <u>Sharon</u> ran home.

A hers

B his

C she

D he

Answer:

C she

---

9 <u>Karl</u> dropped the ball.

A His

B Him

C She

D He

---

10 Have you seen <u>Heather's</u> book?

A his

B her

C hers

D she

GO

11 Where did Troy put <u>his bike</u>?

   A he

   B she

   C it

   D them

---

12 Are <u>Katie and Kelly</u> twins?

   A they

   B them

   C she

   D hers

Directions for Questions 13 to 16: Read each sentence and then choose the correct sentence to go with it.

Example: Are you going to Sarah's house to play?

   A No, I'm not washing the dishes.

   B Yes, I'm going there right after school.

   C Yes, I'm four feet tall.

   D No, I hate vegetables.

Answer:

   B Yes, I'm going there right after school.

---

13 Does Paula like ice cream?

   A Yes, she likes it very much.

   B Yes, she went there yesterday.

   C No, she goes to the other school.

   D No, that is on the next street.

---

14 I do not see Jeffrey's puppy.

   A Sandra sang a nice song.

   B No, but he likes vanilla.

   C He did that yesterday.

   D There it is next to the steps.

---

15 Jonas does not look like his mother.

   A Linda is older than her sister Kim.

   B He tried that yesterday.

   C He has blonde hair, but his mother has black hair.

   D It made him ill.

---

16 I forgot to sweep the steps today.

   A I will do it tomorrow.

   B I did it today.

   C It did not hurt.

   D They are nice and clean now.

Directions for Questions 17 to 20:
Look at the sentences. They tell about the same thing. Then look at the choices and choose the sentence that also tells about the same thing.

Example: Dinosaurs were giant creatures. They lived a long time ago.

    A Scientists collect their bones.

    B Susie likes to fish.

    C They eat spaghetti for lunch.

    D Harold reads very well.

Answer:

    A Scientists collect their bones.

---

17 Baxter, Biscuit, and Sparkey are puppies. They live in a big house. They have a boy and a girl to play with.

    A My friend Melissa has a pet snake.

    B Arthur's father is painting the house.

    C They chase cats for fun.

    D Why did Daddy smile when he opened the letter?

---

18 The Eastern Diamondback rattlesnake is a very large snake. It lives among rocks on the side of hills.

    A The bustard is a funny bird.

    B I am afraid of bats.

    C I camped out in the snow once.

    D It feeds on small birds and mice.

---

19 Ms. Johnson paid Tana to rake her yard. Tana made piles and piles of leaves.

    A Then she put the leaves into bags.

    B Tana likes lemonade.

    C It is almost Thanksgiving.

    D My brother cuts grass.

---

20 Dan stood in the hot beach sand. The waves came in and out. Dan bent down and picked up a shell.

    A The next day, he went home.

    B He held it up to his ear and thought he could hear the ocean in it.

    C He lives in Springfield with his parents.

    D He has a little sister named Arla.

GO ⇨

Directions for Questions 21 to 25: Choose the sentences that are written correctly.

Example:

   A Sally likes, to play with dolls?

   B Sally likes to play, with dolls.

   C Sally likes to play with dolls.

   D Sally, likes to play with dolls.

Answer:

   C Sally likes to play with dolls.

---

21 **A** Peaches, grow on trees, but Grapes grow on vines.

     B Peaches grow on trees, but grapes grow on vines.

     C Peaches grow. On trees but grapes grow on vines.

     D Peaches grow, on trees, but grapes grow on vines.

---

22 **A** One puppy is good, and two puppies are better, but three puppies are best.

     B One puppy is good and two puppies are better but three puppies are best.

     C One puppy is good, and, two puppies are better, but, three puppies are best.

     D One, puppy, is good, and two, puppies, are better, but three puppies are best.

---

23 **A** Whose football, broke my window.

     B Whose football broke my window.

     C Whose football broke my window?

     D Whose football broke! my window!

---

24 **A** My puppy sparky is brown, and white.

     B My puppy Sparky is brown and white.

     C My Puppy sparky is brown and white.

     D My puppy Sparky is brown, and white.

---

25 **A** My brother found him's keys.

     B My brother found its keys.

     C My brother found hisen keys.

     D My brother found his keys.

STOP

SPELLING

Directions for Questions 1 to 13: Look at the words. Choose the word that is spelled <u>correctly</u>.

Example:

- **A** orse
- **B** hrose
- **C** horse
- **D** hrse

Answer:

- **C** horse

1 **A** barn
  B bahrn
  C banr
  D nrab

2 **A** kye
  B kee
  C key
  D kii

3 **A** bott
  B boht
  C bote
  D boat

4 **A** frma
  B farm
  C fmar
  D marf

5 **A** thenk
  B think
  C thinck
  D thynk

6 **A** teacher
  B teecher
  C ticher
  D toocher

7 **A** poosh
  B pushe
  C push
  D possh

8 **A** hend
  B hand
  C hynd
  D hund

GO

9 A dogg

B dog

C dawg

D doge

10 A litul

B litle

C littel

D little

11 A boy

B boye

C boyy

D boi

12 A kepe

B keap

C keepe

D keep

13 A carr

B khar

C kahr

D car

Directions for Questions 14 to 25:
Look at the words. Choose the word that is NOT spelled correctly.

Example:

A fear

B cat

C kittn

D pony

Answer:

C kittn

14 A love

B loaf

C luv

D leaf

15 A head

B heed

C hedd

D hard

16 A apple

B April

C about

D appul

GO

17 **A** took

    B take

    C tuk

    D tale

18 **A** boat

    B bote

    C bat

    D bait

19 **A** lady

    B ladee

    C late

    D left

20 **A** ran

    B run

    C roam

    D runn

21 **A** tell

    B tale

    C tel

    D told

22 **A** made

    B maed

    C maid

    D meet

23 **A** four

    B flower

    C floor

    D flore

24 **A** best

    B beast

    C boast

    D beste

25 **A** right

    B ride

    C rite

    D rit

STOP

MATH CONCEPTS

1 Which card has eight diamonds?

A  **B**  **C**  **D**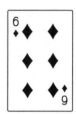

2 Choose the object with four wheels.

A  **B**  **C**  **D**

3 Choose the word and numeral that go together.

A nine 9 **B** six 5 **C** four 7 **D** three 5

4 Choose the word that goes with the number 7.

A eleven **B** seven **C** five **D** two

5 Choose the answer in which the numeral tells the number of items in the picture.

A 1 **B** 5  **C** 3  **D** 4

6 How many pencils are there in this picture?

A 9	**B** 8
C 7	**D** 3

7 Choose the number that is more than 8.

A 7	**B** 6
C 9	**D** 3

8 Choose the answer in which the numbers are in the <u>wrong</u> order, either from least to most, or most to least.

A 2, 6, 8, 9	**B** 9, 7, 3, 1
C 4, 8, 3, 5	**D** 3, 4, 5, 6

9 How many dots are there in this picture?

A 8	**B** 4
C 12	**D** 16

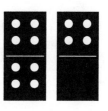

10 How many spots are on the two dominos altogether?

A 9

B 12

C 16

D 8

11 Which animal is third from the left?

A cat

B puppy

C bear

D turtle

12 Which number is third?
8, 1, 3, 5, 9

A 5

B 1

C 8

D 3

13 How much of the pie has been cut?

A one-third   **B** one-fourth   **C** one-fifth   **D** one-eighth

14 There are eight children at Mara's birthday party. Half of the children who came were girls. How many were boys?

A 4   **B** 2   **C** 6   **D** 8

15 Which card has the same number as the number of kittens in the picture above?

A    **B**    **C**    **D**

16 Amy planted pumpkins. If each plant grew one pumpkin, how many pumpkins did she grow?

A 12   **B** 5   **C** 6   **D** 10

17 The number is 852. Which number is in the tens place?

   A 8

   B 5

   C 6

   D 2

18 The number is 291. How many hundreds are in this number?

   A two

   B nine

   C one

   D seven

19 We will count by threes. Fill in the blank: 3, 6, 9, __, 15

   A 11

   B 12

   C 13

   D 9

20 We will count by twos. Fill in the blank: 2, 4, 6, __, 10.

   A 7

   B 9

   C 8

   D 10

21 Choose the sentence that is true about the picture above.

   A The box is over the bear.

   B The bear is standing beside the box.

   C The bear is standing behind the box.

   D The bear is standing on the box.

22 If we want to <u>add</u> 2 and 3, fill in the blank: 2 __ 3 = 5.

   A −

   B +

   C =

   D <

23 If we want to subtract 4 from six, fill in the blank: 6 − 4 __ 2.

   A −

   B +

   C =

   D *

GO

24 Which tree has the most apples?

A  B  C  D

25 Choose the smallest number.

A 11 **B** 16 **C** 12 **D** 8

STOP

MATH COMPUTATION

Directions: Try to solve these problems. If a problem is too hard, it is all right to skip it and come back to it later.

Example:

```
  3
+2
```

A 1

B 5

C 6

D 4

Answer:

B 5

1
```
  7
+5
```

A 2

B 5

C 12

D 7

2
```
  9
−4
```

A 13

B 4

C 5

D 3

3
```
 11
+11
```

A 22

B 13

C 12

D 21

4
```
18
−6
```

A 14

B 24

C 12

D 2

GO→

5 14 + 5 = __

A 19

B 9

C 5

D 15

6 8 − 3 = __

A 4

B 5

C 6

D 7

7 18
   −2

A 16

B 6

C 12

D 14

8 11
   +8

A 19

B 9

C 17

D 7

9 4 + 3 = __

A 9

B 8

C 7

D 1

10 10
   −3

A 6

B 13

C 5

D 7

Cut along dashed line.

GO

11 12
   +3

   A 16

   B 11

   C 19

   D 15

12 9 – __ = 6

   A 4

   B 5

   C 3

   D 2

13 4 + __ = 9

   A 6

   B 5

   C 4

   D 2

14 7
   +7

   A 14

   B 77

   C 11

   D 21

15 19
   −11

   A 12

   B 8

   C 80

   D 6

16 4 + 3 + 1 = __

   A 8

   B 23

   C 9

   D 11

17   2
    3
  <u>+5</u>

  A 10

  B 15

  C 8

  D 9

18   33
  <u>−22</u>

  A 10

  B 12

  C 8

  D 11

19   23
  <u>+23</u>

  A 36

  B 55

  C 46

  D 42

20   32
  <u>−10</u>

  A 12

  B 22

  C 42

  D 9

21 $16 - 7 = $ ___

  A 12

  B 10

  C 11

  D 9

22 $12 - 2 = $ ___

  A 8

  B 14

  C 10

  D 16

GO

Cut along dashed line.

23 26 + 12 = ___

    A 38

    B 28

    C 48

    D 58

24 10
   −1

    A 9

    B 8

    C 7

    D 11

25 29
   −23

    A 17

    B 12

    C 6

    D 9

STOP

MATH APPLICATIONS

1 Ben's mother sent him to the store for 4 pounds of peanuts. What did Ben use to make sure he bought exactly 4 pounds of peanuts?

A 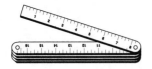   **B**    **C**   **D**

---

2 The sailor needed cloth for a new sail. How did he measure the amount of cloth he needed?

A grams   **B** gallons   **C** yards   **D** liters

---

3 What is the shape of a basketball?

A square   **B** oval   **C** cone   **D** sphere

---

4 How many sides are there in a triangle?

A 4   **B** 3   **C** 2   **D** 5

5 Choose the picture that has the same shape as the drawing above.

A    **B**   **C**    **D**

GO ▷

November

Sunday	Monday	Tuesday	Wednesday	Thursday	Friday	Saturday
			1	2	3	4
5	6	7	8	9	10	11
12	13	14	15	16	17	18
19	20	21	22	(23)	24	25
26	27	28	29	30		

6 Bob's birthday is November 23. What day of the week will his birthday be?

A Wednesday

B Friday

C Thursday

D Sunday

7 Bob had his birthday party on the Saturday before his birthday. What date did he have his birthday party?

A November 12

B November 25

C November 18

D November 30

8 Lisa read six books during summer vacation. Her best friend Carol read seven books. How many books did they read in all?

A 12

B 19

C 11

D 13

9 Jane found a board that was 8 feet long. She only needed a board that was 5 feet long. How many feet did she need to cut off?

A 4

B 8

C 5

D 3

10 What time is shown on this clock?

A 2:45

B 3:15

C 9:15

D 9:45

GO

11 Choose the two clocks that tell the same time.

A

B

C

D

12 Thomas called John and invited him to come over to play video games. John left home at 10:20. It took him 15 minutes to walk to Thomas' house. What time did John arrive at Thomas' house?

A 10:50

B 10:35

C 10:45

D 10:30

13 How many minutes different are these clocks?

A 30

B 20

C 40

D 50

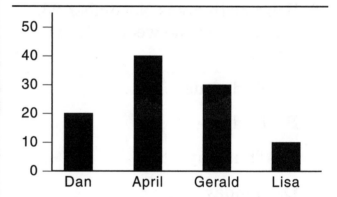

Dan, April, Gerald, and Lisa picked peaches at their grandparents' farm. The chart above shows the number of peaches they picked.

14 How many peaches did Gerald pick?

A 20

B 30

C 40

D 10

GO

Cut along dashed line

15 How many more peaches did Dan pick than Lisa?

   A 20

   B 30

   C They picked the same number of peaches.

   D 10

16 How many peaches did Lisa pick?

   A 20

   B 40

   C 50

   D 10

17 Choose the sentence that is true about the picture.

   A The bicycle is behind the boy.

   B The boy is beside the bicycle.

   C The boy is behind the bicycle.

   D The boy is in front of the bicycle.

18 The cat is on top of the car.

   A

   B

   C

   D
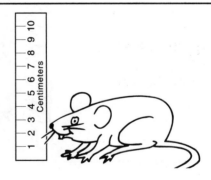

19 How tall is the mouse?

   A 5 inches

   B 5 meters

   C 5 centimeters

   D 5 feet

20 Choose the two that measure the same type of thing.

    A   meters and pounds

    B   ounces and centimeters

    C   gallons and pounds

    D   liters and gallons

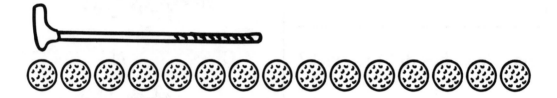

21 How many golf balls long is this golf club?

    A   7   **B**   10   **C**   5   **D**   15

22 How many mice tall is the cat?

    A   4   **B**   9   **C**   10   **D**   6

23 Grandpa baked a blueberry pie. He wanted to divide it equally among himself, Dawn, Linda, and Bill. If he wanted to give everyone the same amount, how much of the pie should he cut for each person?

    A   one-half   **B**   four-fourths   **C**   two-fourths   **D**   one-fourth

24 How much are these coins worth in all?

A 40 cents **B** 20 cents

C one dollar **D** 50 cents

25 Jamal bought a newspaper for 25 cents. The cashier added 3 cents sales tax. How much did he pay for the newspaper in all?

A 25 cents

B 28 cents

C 30 cents

D one quarter

STOP

Answer Key for Sample Practice Test

Word Analysis

1	C
2	B
3	D
4	D
5	B
6	A
7	B
8	D
9	A
10	A
11	C
12	B
13	D
14	D
15	B
16	A
17	D
18	B
19	C
20	C
21	B
22	C
23	B
24	A
25	A

Vocabulary

1	D
2	C
3	A
4	D
5	D
6	B

7	D
8	A
9	A
10	A
11	D
12	B
13	A
14	D
15	B
16	D
17	D
18	A
19	C
20	A
21	B
22	A
23	D
24	B
25	B

Reading Comprehension

1	A
2	C
3	D
4	C
5	C
6	B
7	A
8	D
9	D
10	D
11	D
12	D

13	A
14	A
15	D
16	B
17	A
18	D
19	B
20	A
21	D
22	D
23	B
24	A
25	B

Listening

1	C
2	A
3	B
4	D
5	B
6	A
7	C
8	B
9	C
10	B
11	A
12	D
13	A
14	B
15	C
16	D
17	D
18	D
19	D

20	B
21	D
22	D
23	A
24	C
25	C

Language Mechanics

1	B
2	A
3	B
4	D
5	D
6	B
7	A
8	A
9	D
10	B
11	C
12	A
13	A
14	D
15	C
16	A
17	C
18	D
19	A
20	B
21	B
22	A
23	C
24	B
25	D

Spelling		**Math Concepts**		**Math Computation**		**Math Applications**	
1	A	1	A	1	C	1	B
2	C	2	C	2	C	2	C
3	D	3	A	3	A	3	D
4	B	4	B	4	C	4	B
5	B	5	A	5	A	5	A
6	A	6	B	6	B	6	C
7	C	7	C	7	A	7	C
8	B	8	C	8	A	8	D
9	B	9	D	9	C	9	D
10	D	10	B	10	D	10	C
11	A	11	A	11	D	11	A
12	D	12	D	12	C	12	B
13	D	13	B	13	B	13	C
14	C	14	A	14	A	14	B
15	C	15	B	15	B	15	D
16	D	16	C	16	A	16	D
17	C	17	B	17	A	17	B
18	B	18	A	18	D	18	C
19	B	19	B	19	C	19	C
20	D	20	C	20	B	20	D
21	C	21	D	21	D	21	A
22	B	22	B	22	C	22	D
23	D	23	C	23	A	23	D
24	D	24	C	24	A	24	D
25	D	25	D	25	C	25	B